CONTINUOUS MEASUREMENT OF BLOOD OXYGEN SATURATION IN THE HIGH RISK PATIENT

Volume 1

Proceedings of a seminar entitled "Is Continuous Measurement of Blood Oxygen Saturation a Significant Advance in Hemodynamic Monitoring and Management of the High Risk Patient?" held June 4, 1982 in conjunction with the Eleventh Annual Scientific and Educational Symposium of The Society of Critical Care Medicine in St. Louis, Missouri.

Editor
John F. Schweiss, M.D.

Beach International, Inc.
San Diego, California

This publication was sponsored under an educational grant from **Oximetrix, Inc.**

Beach International, Inc.
P.O. Box 28364
11858 Bernardo Plaza Court
San Diego, California 92128

Distributed by
Oximetrix, Inc.
1212 Terra Bella Avenue
Mountain View, California 94043

Library of Congress Catalog
Number 82-074046

International Standard Book
Number 0-942210-20-4

Printed in the United States
of America

PREFACE

Hemodynamic monitoring is essential to the management of cardiopulmonary performance in the high risk patient. Although intermittent *in vivo* blood gas analysis has been available, its clinical utility has been limited. Now, technological advances have brought continuous measurement of blood oxygen saturation, in general, and mixed venous oxygen saturation ($S\bar{v}O_2$), in particular, to the forefront of clinical scientific interest.

This monograph is a compilation of papers presented at the Eleventh Annual Scientific and Educational Symposium of the Society of Critical Care Medicine in St. Louis, Missouri on June 4, 1982 at a seminar entitled "Is Continuous Measurement Of Blood Oxygen Saturation A Significant Advance in Hemodynamic Monitoring And Management Of The High Risk Patient?"

The relationship of hemodynamic theory to practice is examined by outstanding critical care physicians, as they present their clinical observations of continuous oxygen saturation monitoring. Topics discussed include oxygen transport physiology, blood oxygen chemistry in the critical care patient and the relationship of mixed venous oxygen saturation to cardiac output and other hemodynamic variables. The issue of *in vivo* versus *in vitro* blood oxygen measurement is evaluated in terms of both accuracy and cost-effectiveness. The clinical utility of continuous oxygen measurement is assessed for intraoperative, postoperative and intensive care uses.

This monograph makes available for your reading and reference the most recent research and thinking in the critical care field concerning continuous measurement of blood oxygen saturation and its use in assessment and management of the high risk patient.

John F. Schweiss, M.D.
Professor and Chairman
Department of Anesthesiology
St. Louis University School of Medicine
St. Louis, Missouri

PRESENTERS

Arnold Aberman, M.D.
Professor of Medicine
University of Toronto
Physician-in-Chief
Mount Sinai Hospital
Toronto, Ontario, Canada

Patrick J. Fahey, M.D.
Assistant Professor of Medicine
and Anesthesiology
Director, Medical Intensive Care Unit
Pulmonary Division
Foster G. McGaw Hospital
Loyola University of Chicago
Maywood, Illinois

John W. Hoyt, M.D.
Assistant Professor of Anesthesiology
and Medical Director, Intensive Care Unit
University of Virginia Medical Center
Charlottesville, Virginia

Arnold S. Leonard, M.D., Ph.D.
Professor of Surgery
Head, Pediatric Surgery Service
Head, Computer Patient Monitoring
University of Minnesota Hospitals
Minneapolis, Minnesota

John C. McMichan, M.B., B.S., Ph.D., F.C.C.P.
Consultant in Intensive Care and Anesthesiology
Mayo Clinic
Assistant Professor of Anesthesiology
Mayo Medical School
Director, Surgical and Trauma Intensive Care Unit
St. Mary's Hospital
Rochester, Minnesota

Philip A. Poole-Wilson, M.D., M.R.C.P.
Reader in Cardiology and Vice Dean
Cardiothoracic Institute
Honorary Consultant Physician
National Heart Hospital
London, England

John F. Schweiss, M.D.
Professor and Chairman
Department of Anesthesiology
St. Louis University School of Medicine
Chief of Anesthesiology
Cardinal Glennon Memorial Hospital for Children
Firmin Desloge Hospital and St. Louis City Hospital
St. Louis, Missouri

Curtis A. Sheldon, M.D.
Fellow in General Surgery
University of Minnesota Hospitals
Minneapolis, Minnesota

CONTRIBUTORS

Rudolph Canepa-Anson, M.D.
Senior Registrar
National Heart Hospital
London, England

Charles G. Durbin, Jr., M.D.
Assistant Professor of Anesthesiology
University of Virginia Medical Center
Charlottesville, Virginia

H. David McLachlan, B.S.
Supervisor, Cardiovascular Monitoring Technicians
Surgical Intensive Care Unit
University of Virginia Medical Center
Charlottesville, Virginia

Frank D. Sottile, M.D.
Fellow in Anesthesiology
Department of Anesthesiology
University of Virginia Medical Center
Charlottesville, Virginia

Robert F. Swain, B.S., R.R.T.
Cardiovascular Monitoring Technician
University of Virginia Medical Center
Charlottesville, Virginia

TABLE OF CONTENTS

Chapter One 1
INTRODUCTION AND HISTORICAL PERSPECTIVE
John F. Schweiss, M.D.

Chapter Two 13
FUNDAMENTALS OF OXYGEN TRANSPORT PHYSIOLOGY IN A HEMODYNAMIC MONITORING CONTEXT
Arnold Aberman, M.D., F.A.C.P.

Chapter Three 27
CONTINUOUS MONITORING OF MIXED VENOUS OXYGEN SATURATION
THEORY APPLIED TO PRACTICE
John C. McMichan, M.B., B.S., Ph.D., F.C.C.P.

Chapter Four 45
CONTINUOUS $S\bar{v}O_2$ AS PREDICTOR OF CHANGES IN CARDIAC OUTPUT: CLINICAL OBSERVATIONS
John W. Hoyt, M.D.
Frank D. Sottile, M.D.
Charles G. Durbin, Jr., M.D.
Robert F. Swain, B.S., R.R.T.
H. David McLachlan, B.S.

Chapter Five 59
CONTINUOUS MEASUREMENT OF CORONARY SINUS OXYGEN SATURATION AS A METHOD FOR DETECTING CORONARY ARTERY DISEASE
Philip A. Poole-Wilson, M.D., M.R.C.P.
Rudolph Canepa-Anson, M.D.

Chapter Six 67
CONTINUOUS $S\bar{v}O_2$ AND OTHER NEW HEMODYNAMIC PARAMETERS AS EARLY INDICATORS OF HYPOVOLEMIA
Curtis A. Sheldon, M.D.
Arnold S. Leonard, M.D., Ph.D.

Chapter Seven 81
USE OF CONTINUOUS $S\bar{v}O_2$ INTRA AND POSTOPERATIVELY IN MANAGING THE HEMODYNAMICS OF CARDIAC SURGERY PATIENTS
John F. Schweiss, M.D.

Chapter Eight 113
AN OVERALL CLINICAL ASSESSMENT OF THE ROLE OF CONTINUOUS $S\bar{v}O_2$ MEASUREMENT IN HEMODYNAMIC MONITORING IN THE ICU
Patrick J. Fahey, M.D.

Chapter Nine 123
IS CONTINUOUS MEASUREMENT OF BLOOD OXYGEN SATURATION A SIGNIFICANT ADVANCE IN HEMODYNAMIC MONITORING AND MANAGEMENT OF THE HIGH RISK PATIENT?

PANEL DISCUSSION
QUESTIONS AND ANSWERS

Arnold Aberman, M.D., F.A.C.P.
Patrick J. Fahey, M.D.
John W. Hoyt, M.D.
Arnold S. Leonard, M.D.
John C. McMichan, M.D., B.S., Ph.D.
Philip A. Poole-Wilson, M.D., M.R.C.P.
John F. Schweiss, M.D.
Curtis A. Sheldon, M.D.

INTRODUCTION AND HISTORICAL PERSPECTIVE

1

John F. Schweiss, M.D.*

As you may be aware, this conference has been developed and sponsored by Oximetrix, Inc., a company which has persisted in the field of *in vivo* oximetry. This is not a new concept, but the practical aspects of widespread clinical usage have eluded previous technology and manufacturing expertise.

This ability to measure and record mixed venous oxygen saturation ($S\bar{v}O_2$) *in vivo* continuously has recently become clinically available in a reliable fiberoptic reflectance oximetry system incorporated in a 5 Lumen 7.5 Fr. balloon-tipped, thermodilution, pulmonary artery catheter. This catheter interfaces with a microprocessor-based instrument that utilizes an improved spectrophotometric technique involving the use of light emitting diodes, providing light signals at three different wavelengths in the red and infrared light spectrum. The instrument has a continuous strip chart recorder, and digital display and alarm limits. This system is an outgrowth of a three-wavelength 4 Fr. umbilical artery catheter oximetry system introduced by Oximetrix in 1977.

*St. Louis University School of Medicine
Section on Anesthesiology (Surgery)
1325 South Grand Boulevard
St. Louis, Missouri 63104

Historically, the hemoreflector developed by Brinkmann and Zijstra in 1949 demonstrated the ability of reflection oximetry to monitor oxygen saturation.[1]

Boyd, Bahnson, et al reported in 1959 that cardiac output determinations in the postoperative period following cardiopulmonary bypass correlated best with $S\bar{v}O_2$.[2] The latter determination of $S\bar{v}O_2$, according to the authors, gave more information than any other single determination.

A reflection type oximeter was developed by Polyanyi and Hehir in 1961.[3] This unit, commercially manufactured by the American Optical Company, utilized two wavelengths: 805 nm and 650 nm. They established that equal reliability, as shown in Figure 1, could be obtained with reflection oximetry when compared to the more cumbersome techniques of Van Slyke and Beckmann, which utilized hemolyzed blood. The reflectance system utilized whole blood, and made possible the bedside evaluation of oxygen saturation on multiple samples drawn from indwelling catheters.

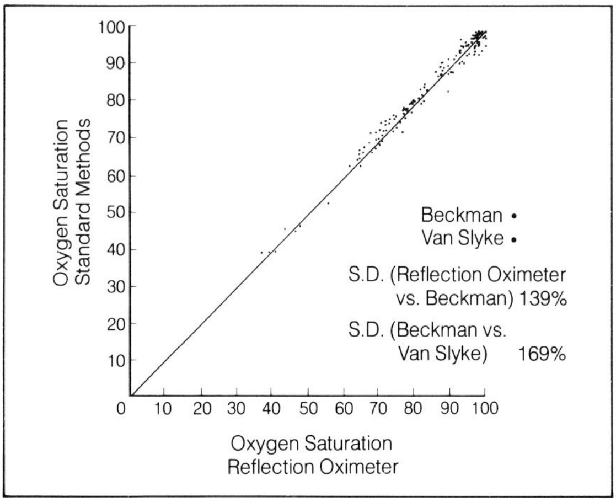

Figure 1*

The first research system providing continuous recording of blood oxygen saturation, utilizing a Clark oxygen electrode, was reported by McArthur, Clark, et al.[4] They once again established, as early as 1962, the value of continuous mixed venous oxygen content or saturation as the earliest sign of hemodynamic competence or incompetence.

*Reprinted with permission from Journal of Thoracic and Cardiovascular Surgery. Ware P.F. Polyani M.L., Hehir R.M., et al: A new reflection oximeter. J. Thoracic and C.V. Surgery, 42:580-588, 1961.

Muir et al, in 1970, related $S\bar{v}O_2$ to cardiac output in patients with acute myocardial infarction and compared individuals whose courses were uncomplicated with those who showed evidence of left ventricular failure and those in obvious cardiogenic shock.[5] They compared cardiac output obtained by dye dilution techniques, and demonstrated good correlation between cardiac index and $S\bar{v}O_2$ obtained from a float-in catheter in the pulmonary artery, as shown in Figure 2. Oxygen saturations were derived from the data of Severinghaus from blood gas data obtained on a Model 113 Blood Gas Analyzer of Instrumentation Laboratories.

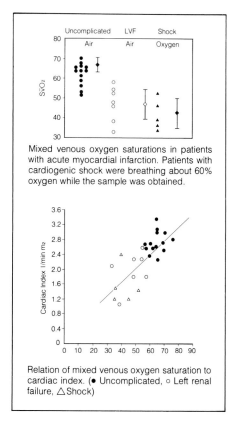

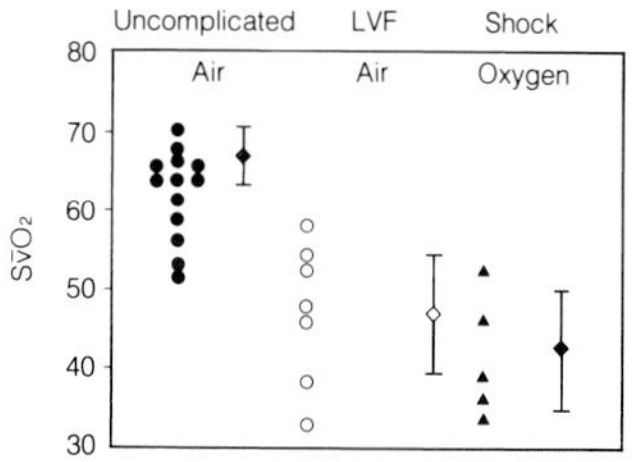

Mixed venous oxygen saturations in patients with acute myocardial infarction. Patients with cardiogenic shock were breathing about 60% oxygen while the sample was obtained.

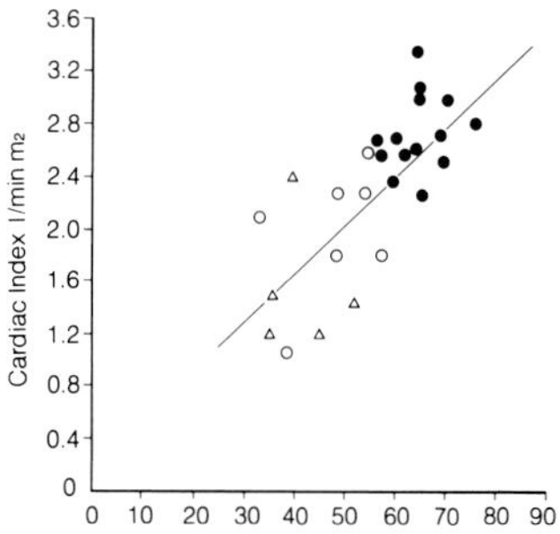

Relation of mixed venous oxygen saturation to cardiac index. (● Uncomplicated, ○ Left renal failure, △ Shock)

Figure 2*

*Reprinted with permission from British Medical Journal. Muir A.L., Kirby B.S., King A.J., Miller H.C.: Mixed venous oxygen saturation in relation to cardiac output in myocardial infarction. British Medical Journal 4:276-278, 1970.

Cole, Johnson and Martin, at the University of Washington in 1972, developed a system incorporating a two wavelength system in a polyethylene catheter, 7 Fr. in diameter. They established the feasibility of fiberoptic catheter oximetry, as shown in Figure 3.

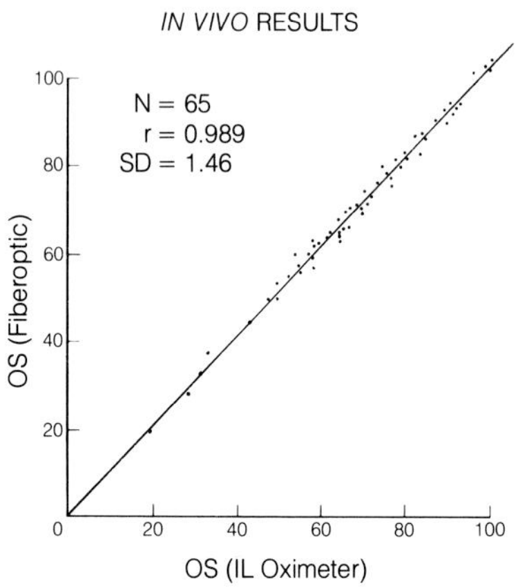

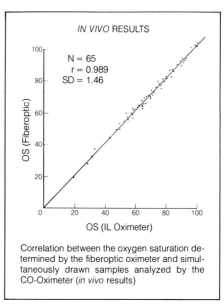

Correlation between the oxygen saturation determined by the fiberoptic oximeter and simultaneously drawn samples analyzed by the CO-Oximeter (*in vivo* results)

Figure 3*

The commercial development of their system by Physio-Control, utilizing a fiberoptic Swan-Ganz® catheter manufactured by Edwards Laboratories, failed to be clinically accepted due to difficulties in standardizing, *in vivo* calibration, drift, catheter stiffness, wall artifact and clot formation. This Physio-Control/Edwards Laboratories fiberoptic system utilized a 100 filament bundle for transmission of the two wavelengths of light to and from the tip of the catheter.

*Reprinted with permission from American Journal of Cardiology. Cole J.S., Martin W.E., Chung P.W., Johnson C.C.: Clinical studies with a solid state fiberoptic oximeter. American J. Card. 29:383-388, 1972.

In 1975 Parr and Kirklin reported on their experiences in measuring cardiac index and $S\bar{v}O_2$, and plotted these values in relationship to the probability of acute cardiac deaths. You will note that the solid line, which represents the cardiac index in Figure 4, parallels very closely the $S\bar{v}O_2$ curve shown in the figure.

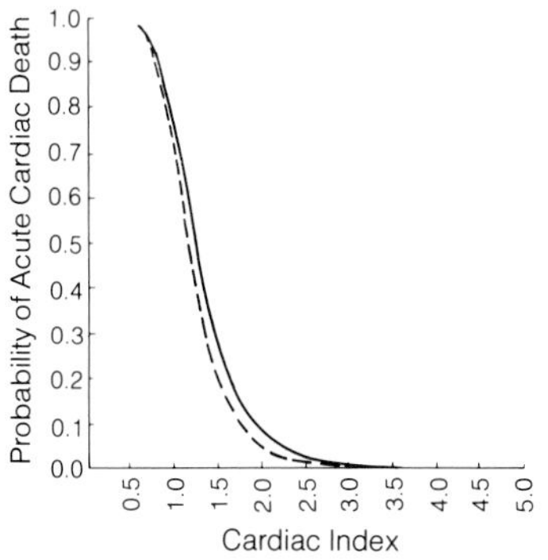

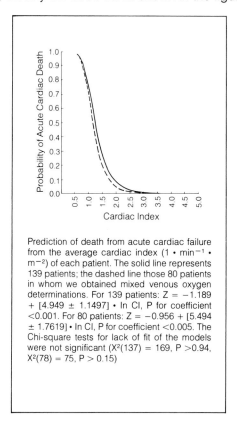

Prediction of death from acute cardiac failure from the average cardiac index ($1 \cdot min^{-1} \cdot m^{-2}$) of each patient. The solid line represents 139 patients; the dashed line those 80 patients in whom we obtained mixed venous oxygen determinations. For 139 patients: $Z = -1.189 + [4.949 \pm 1.1497] \cdot \ln CI$, P for coefficient <0.001. For 80 patients: $Z = -0.956 + [5.494 \pm 1.7619] \cdot \ln CI$, P for coefficient <0.005. The Chi-square tests for lack of fit of the models were not significant ($X^2(137) = 169$, $P > 0.94$, $X^2(78) = 75$, $P > 0.15$)

Figure 4*

In 1977 Oximetrix introduced a catheter oximeter system with a fiberoptic umbilical artery catheter. This system incorporated an improved spectrophotometric design utilizing three judiciously selected wavelengths, instead of the two that were used in previous systems. This three-wavelength technology resulted in an improved instrument with less sensitivity to changes in hematocrit, blood pH, blood flow and temperature. In 1981 a fiberoptic thermodilution pulmonary artery catheter was introduced for use with this system. The use of plastic monofilaments as the fiberoptic transmitter and

*Reprinted with permission from Circulation. Parr G.V.S., Blackstone E.H., Kirklin J.W.: Cardiac performance and mortality after intracardiac surgery in infants and children. Circulation 51:867, 1975.

receiver allowed the fiberoptic catheters to retain much of the flexibility and handling characteristics of conventional thermodilution pulmonary artery catheters. This has resulted in a catheter with clinical acceptance that has proven to be reliable in clinical use. Figure 5 shows the instrument that is used with this catheter with its visual readout and continuous recording system, and the original pulmonary artery catheter with its balloon inflated.

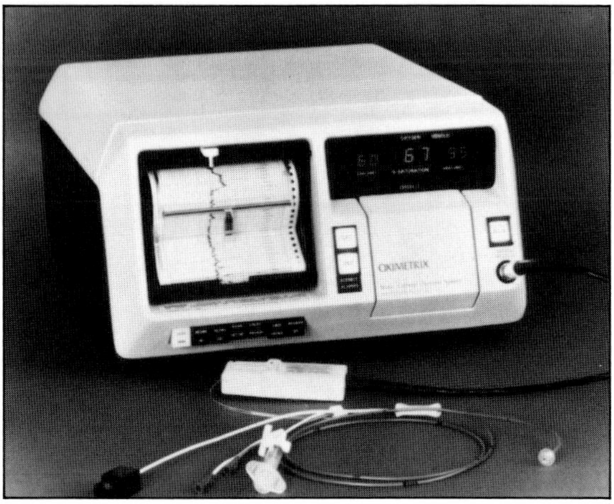

Figure 5

An improved pulmonary artery catheter design was introduced in January, 1982. The improved design has better catheter tip curvature and greater flexibility. The flexibility of this new fiberoptic catheter is equivalent to the conventional thermodilution catheter, giving it handling characteristics comparable to the conventional thermodilution catheter, which has facilitated passage into the pulmonary artery.

Baele, McMichan, et al in 1981 confirmed the accuracy, reliability and stability of this Oximetrix pulmonary artery catheter oximetry system by comparing *in vivo* values with samples obtained simultaneously and analyzed on the IL 282 Co-Oximeter, as shown in Figures 6 and 6A.

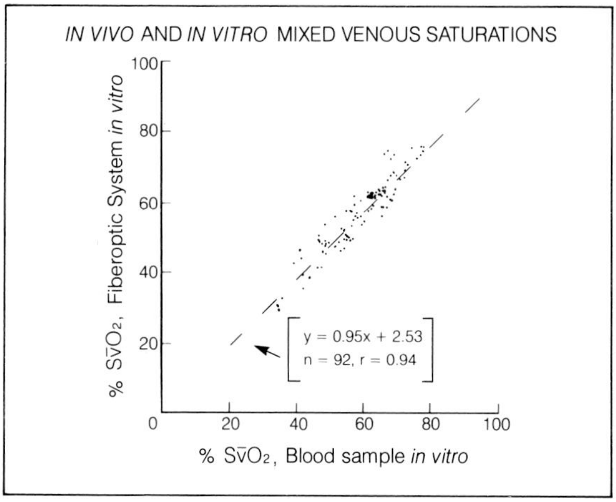

Figure 6*

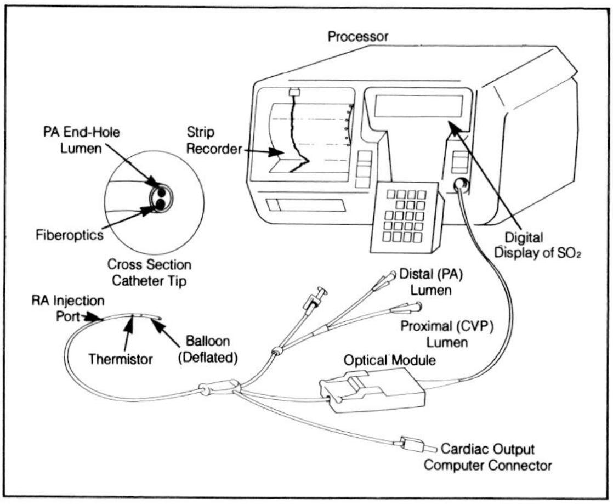

Figure 6A

*Reprinted with permission from Anesthesiology. Baele P.L., McMichan J.C., Marsh M.B., Sill J.C., Southorn P.A.: Continuous monitoring of mixed venous saturation in critically ill patients. Anesthesiology, 55:A113, 1981.

The principle involved in this system is that the ratio of hemoglobin to oxyhemoglobin can be obtained from the relative absorption of light by hemoglobin and oxyhemoglobin at different wavelengths. This is a result of the different light absorption characteristics between hemoglobin and oxyhemoglobin, as illustrated in Figure 7.

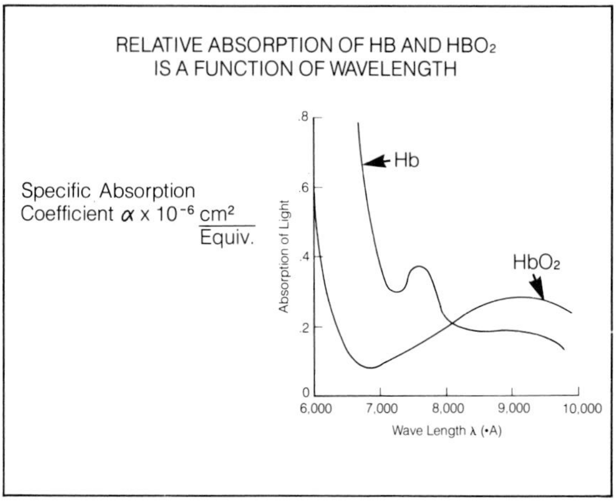

Figure 7

This basic principle is not new to clinical medicine. As illustrated in Figure 8, the conventional benchtop co-oximeter utilizes this principle of different absorption characteristics of oxyhemoglobin at different wavelengths of light using transmission spectrophotometry through a blood sample in a cuvette.

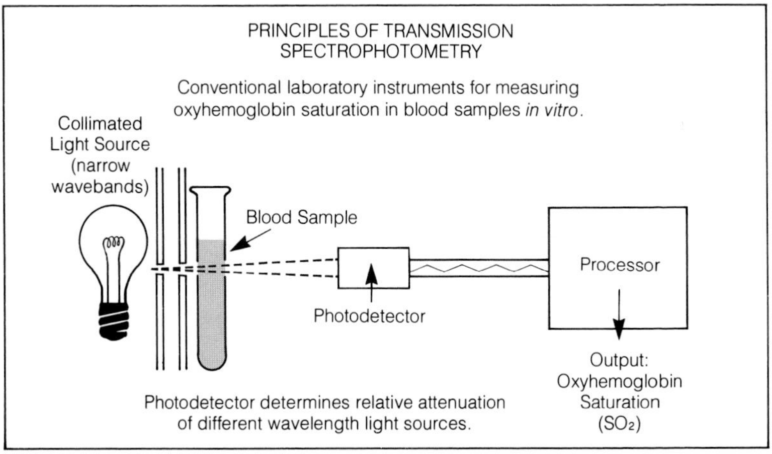

Figure 8

The way that reflectance spectrophotometry is implemented in the catheter oximeter is illustrated in Figure 9. The optical module contains the sources of light which are transmitted to the blood via the fiberoptic monofilament and reflected back in a separate fiberoptic monofilament to the photodetector in the module. The light in turn is electrically transmitted to the microprocessor, whose output is recorded as percent saturation of oxyhemoglobin. The electrical signals from the photodetector are transmitted via the attached cable to the microprocessor. Digital processing of the electronic signals is used to filter out vessel wall artifact interference. The processed signals are then used to calculate the blood oxygen saturation.

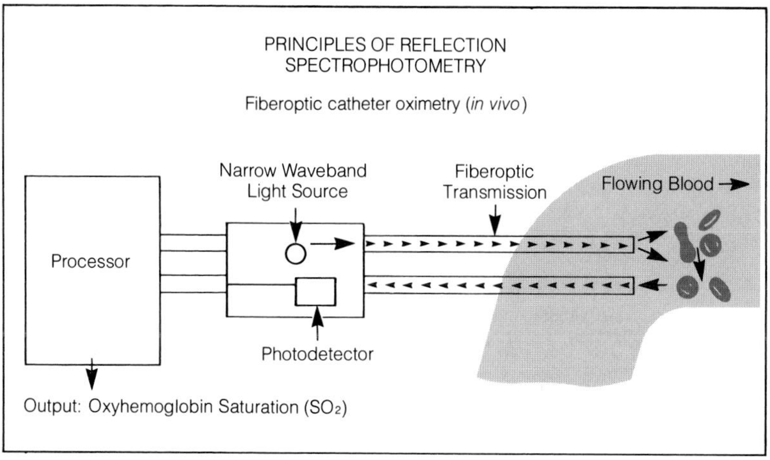

Figure 9

The average $S\bar{v}O_2$ for the preceding five seconds is displayed, and this computation updated every five seconds. Alarms for high and low values can be selected on the keyboard which is located below the numerical displays. The intensity of the reflectance signal is monitored continuously, as well as graphically displayed on the recorder, and can be used to indicate excessive vessel wall artifact and deposits over the optics. The keyboard allows *in vitro* calibration prior to insertion and *in vivo* calibration on blood samples withdrawn from the pulmonary artery tip and analyzed on an IL 282 Co-Oximeter or comparable instrument. This value can be compared with the value noted at the time the sample was withdrawn, and the new value can be inserted by the keyboard.

A derived saturation from a pH and a PO_2 determination utilizing blood gas values can be used, but is less accurate because pH and PO_2 are not the only factors which affect the resultant level of oxyhemoglobin, as shown in Figure 10. The temperature of the blood, the type of hemoglobin, the level of 2,3 DPG and other factors make calculation from blood gas determinations less satisfactory than a direct recording oximeter in terms of accuracy. *In vitro* determinations provide a measure of $S\bar{v}O_2$ intermittently, rather than continuously.

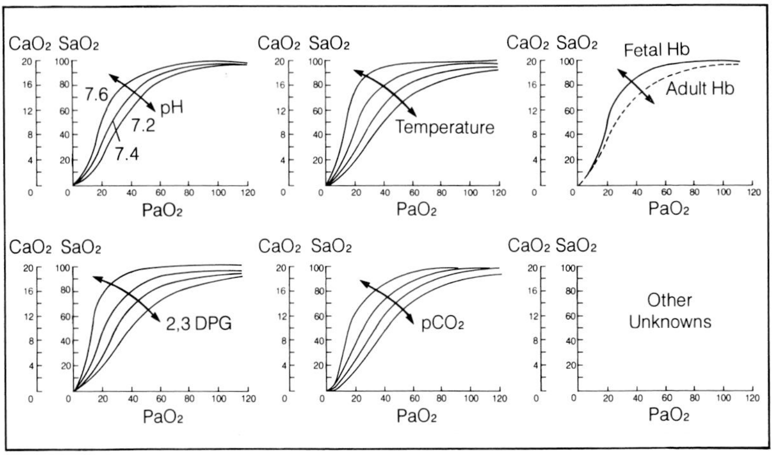

Figure 10

The Oximetrix P7110 fiberoptic catheters, as shown in Figure 11, have all the standard features of previous generation thermodilution pulmonary artery catheters. You will note that the end of the catheter has both an open end lumen for blood sampling and blood pressure monitoring, as well as the two optical fibers which permit the transmission of light and the return of the reflected light to the optical module for transmission to the oximeter.

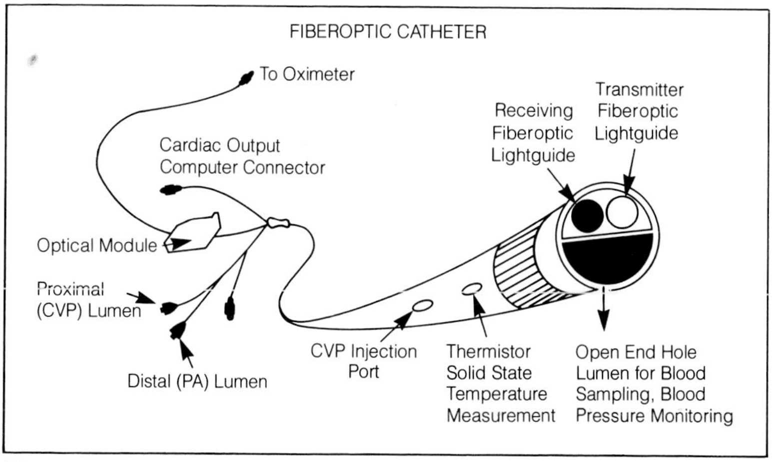

Figure 11

In the chapters to follow, information will be presented on the various aspects of oxygen transport, the relationship of $S\bar{v}O_2$ to cardiac output and other variables, and the clinical utility of continuously monitored and recorded $S\bar{v}O_2$.

REFERENCES

1. Brinkman R. and Zijstra W.G.: Determination and continuous registration of the percentage oxygen saturation in small amounts of blood. Archives Chir. Nuerl. 1:177, 1949.
2. Boyd A.D., Tremblay R.E., Spencer F.C. and Bahnson H.T.: Estimation of cardiac output soon after intra-cardiac surgery with cardiopulmonary bypass. Annals of Surgery 150:613-626, 1959.
3. Ware P.F., Polyani M.L., Hehir R.M., et al: A new reflection oximeter. J. Thoracic and C.V. Surgery 42:580-588, 1961.
4. McArthur K.T., Clark L.C., Lyons C., Edwards S.: Continuous recording of blood oxygen saturation in open heart operations. Surgery 51:121-126, 1962.
5. Muir A.L., Kirby B.J., King A.J., Miller H.C.: Mixed venous oxygen saturation in relation to cardiac output in myocardial infarction. British Medical Journal 4:276-278, 1970.
6. Cole J.S., Martin W.E., Cheung P.W., Johnson C.C.: Clinical studies with a solid state fiberoptic catheter. American J. Card. 29:383-388, 1972.
7. Parr G.V.S., Blackstone E.H., Kirklin, J.W.: Cardiac performance and mortality early after intracardiac surgery in infants and children. Circulation 51:867, 1975.
8. Baele P.L., McMichan J.C., Marsh M.B., Sill J.C., Southorn P.A.: Continuous monitoring of mixed venous saturation in critically ill patients. Anesthesiology 55:A113, 1981.

FUNDAMENTALS OF OXYGEN TRANSPORT PHYSIOLOGY IN A HEMODYNAMIC MONITORING CONTEXT

2

Arnold Aberman, M.D., F.A.C.P.*

This presentation is focused on the fundamentals of oxygen transport physiology in a hemodynamic monitoring context. The oxyhemoglobin dissociation curve will be reviewed, and blood oxygen content, oxygen transport and oxygen consumption will be discussed.

*Mount Sinai Hospital
600 University Avenue, Suite 427
Toronto, Ontario, Canada M5G 1X5

Hemoglobin combines reversibly with oxygen to form oxyhemoglobin. The percent saturation is the amount of oxyhemoglobin over the total amount of hemoglobin, both reduced and oxygenated, as shown in Figure 1.

OXYGEN SATURATION (SO_2)

$$Hb + O_2 \leftrightarrow HbO_2$$

$$SO_2\ (\%) = \frac{HbO_2}{(Hb + HbO_2)} \times 100$$

Figure 1

Saturation is related to PO_2 via the oxyhemoglobin dissociation curve illustrated in Figure 2. This curve should be familiar to most of you, but let me review some important features.

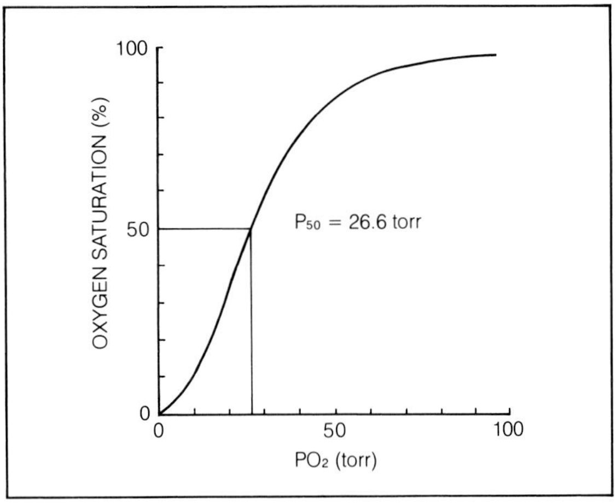

Figure 2

At a normal arterial PO_2 of 90 mmHg the saturation is 97%. If the PO_2 decreases from 90 mmHg to 60 mmHg (a decrease of 33%), the saturation will only decrease from 97% to 92% — a fall of 5%. Thus, on the arterial side saturation is well protected from major changes caused by decreases in arterial PO_2.

On the venous side the picture is somewhat different. The normal venous PO_2 of approximately 40 mmHg has a capillary saturation of 75%. Because of the steep nature of the curve on venous values, small changes in venous PO_2 get translated into large changes in venous saturation. Of course, that has important implications with respect to oxygen unloading at a tissue level.

The next term I want to define is blood oxygen content. Blood oxygen content answers the following question. In 100 ml of blood, how much oxygen is there? As you know, the oxygen exists both dissolved and combined with hemoglobin. The amount dissolved can be estimated by multiplying the PO_2 times .0031, the solubility coefficient. The amount combined with hemoglobin can be estimated by multiplying 1.38 times hemoglobin times saturation, where 1.38 is the maximum, in milliliters oxygen, that one gram of hemoglobin can combine with when fully saturated. In the literature the number ranges from 1.34 to 1.39. In the example illustrated in Figure 3 a normal person with a hemoglobin of 15 gm/dl, a PO_2 of 100 mmHg and a saturation of 97% has 0.3 ml of oxygen dissolved per 100 ml blood. The amount combined with hemoglobin is 20.1 ml, for a total amount of oxygen of 20.4 ml of oxygen per 100 ml of blood.

BLOOD OXYGEN CONTENT (CO_2)

($ml\ O_2/100\ ml\ blood = Vol\ \%$)

O_2 Dissolved + O_2 Combined with Hemoglobin

$$0.0031 \times PO_2 + 1.38 \times Hb \times SO_2$$

Example:

$Hb = 15\ gm\%$, $PO_2 = 100\ mmHg$, $SO_2 = 97\%$

$$CO_2 = (0.0031 \times 100) + (1.38 \times 15 \times .97)$$

$$CO_2 = .3 + 20.1$$

$$CO_2 = 20.4\ Vol\ \%$$

Figure 3

You will notice that the vast majority of oxygen, over 98% in this example, exists combined with hemoglobin. Only a trivial amount is dissolved — less than 2%. Therefore, if you were to ask me what role does PaO_2 play in contributing to oxygen content, I hope you would agree that directly it plays a very minimal role. It is important, of course, but its importance is that PaO_2 is a major determining factor in saturation.

You can estimate oxygen content by ignoring the amount of oxygen dissolved and considering only the amount combined with hemoglobin. Oxygen content can be estimated as simply 1.38 times hemoglobin times saturation. That will introduce only a trivial error in the calculation of content.

Finally, remember that if arterial PaO_2 falls from 100 mmHg to 60 mmHg, a decrease of 40% in this example, saturation only decreases by some 5%. Therefore, if the PaO_2 falls from 100 mmHg to 60 mmHg, content will only fall by some 6-7%, another important clinical point shown in Figure 4.

PaO_2 (mmHg)	SaO_2* (%)	CaO_2** (vol %)
50	85	15.4
60	91	16.4
70	94	17.0
100	97.5	17.6

*pH: 7.40, T: 37°C
**Hb: 13 gm/dl

Figure 4

The next term I want to bring to your attention is oxygen transport. Oxygen transport answers the following question: In a minute, how much oxygen leaves the heart to be delivered to the tissues? You can estimate that value by multiplying the cardiac output (in l/min) times arterial oxygen content (in ml/100 ml blood) times 10. In the example shown in Figure 5, if the patient's cardiac output is 5 l/min and arterial oxygen content is 18 ml/100 ml blood, then every minute 900 ml of oxygen leaves the heart to be delivered to the tissues.

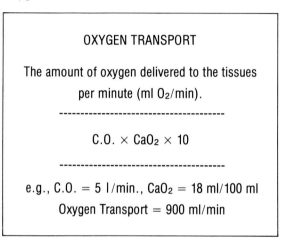

OXYGEN TRANSPORT

The amount of oxygen delivered to the tissues per minute (ml O_2/min).

$$C.O. \times CaO_2 \times 10$$

---

e.g., C.O. = 5 l/min., CaO_2 = 18 ml/100 ml

Oxygen Transport = 900 ml/min

Figure 5

The final term I want to redefine today is oxygen consumption before we move on to consider some aspects of physiology. Oxygen consumption answers the following question: In a minute, how much oxygen is consumed by the body's tissues? If you know the amount of oxygen delivered to the tissues from the heart, arterial oxygen transport, and subtract from that the amount of oxygen that returns from the tissues back to the heart, venous oxygen transport, clearly the difference will be the amount of oxygen consumed by the tissues. We remember that you can represent transport as ten times cardiac output times arterial content; and venous transport as ten times cardiac output times venous content. Factor out the ten as cardiac output, and you come to this very familiar expression: Oxygen consumption is ten times cardiac output times A-V oxygen content difference, as illustrated in Figure 6. Remember, we can estimate content by simply considering the amount combined with hemoglobin and ignoring the amount dissolved. That introduces only a trivial error. Therefore, oxygen consumption can be expressed as: Cardiac output times the hemoglobin times 13.8 times the A-V saturation difference.

O_2 CONSUMPTION (ml O_2/min)

Arterial O_2 Transport − Venous O_2 Transport

$$10 \times C.O. \times CaO_2 - 10 \times C.O. \times C\bar{v}O_2$$

$$10 \times C.O. \times (CaO_2 - C\bar{v}O_2)$$

$$10 \times C.O. \times$$

$$(Hb \times 1.38 \times SaO_2) - (Hb \times 1.38 \times S\bar{v}O_2)$$

$$C.O. \times Hb \times 13.8 \times (SaO_2 - S\bar{v}O_2)$$

Figure 6

If you search for a unifying factor in critically ill patients (patients in shock, whether it is hemorrhagic, septic or cardiogenic), you will find in the literature that lactic acidosis is a common feature. Regardless of the type of shock, when a patient is in end-stage serious shock with an ominous prognosis the blood lactate is almost invariably elevated.

The blood lactate is elevated because the body's oxygen demands are not being met by the oxygen delivery system. In normal people the oxygen consumption must be equal to demand. When that occurs there is no lactic acidosis. When consumption is less than demand in the various types of shock, as shown in Figure 7, lactic acidosis results. Then, unless you can intervene, death will quickly follow.

SHOCK

$$C.O. \times Hb \times 13.8 \times (SaO_2 - S\bar{v}O_2)$$

$$1.6 \times 15 \times 13.8 \times (\ .97 \ - \ .31\ )$$

$$\dot{V}O_2 = 218 \text{ ml/min}$$

Figure 7

Let us look at some normal values for oxygen consumption. With a cardiac output of 5 l/min, a hemoglobin of 15 gm/dl, arterial saturation of 97% and a venous saturation of 75% (all normal values) the oxygen consumption is approximately 228 ml/min, as shown in Figure 8.

NORMAL

$$C.O. \times Hb \times 13.8 \times (SaO_2 - S\bar{v}O_2)$$

$$5 \times 15 \times 13.8 \times (\ .97 \ - \ .75\ )$$

$$\dot{V}O_2 = 228 \text{ ml/min}$$

Figure 8

Weil's group at U.S.C. showed in patients with myocardial infarction resulting from cardiogenic shock, that as the lactate increases (as the patient's oxygen consumption fails to meet tissue oxygen demand) prognosis is dismal.

If we understand that the expression shown in Figure 9 is oxygen consumption; and we understand that it is up to the oxygen delivery system to make sure that oxygen consumption equals demand, we can now ask ourselves two questions. First, in the critically ill patient, what are the factors that can threaten the value of this expression? The three major factors are: A decrease in cardiac output, a decrease in hemoglobin, and a fall in arterial saturation. We will deal with these systematically, shortly.

$$C.O. \times Hb \times 13.8 \times (SaO_2 - S\bar{v}O_2)$$

Figure 9

Before we look at the factors that can threaten the value of this expression, let us ask ourselves a second question: What are the compensatory steps the body can take when the value of this expression is threatened? These compensatory steps will turn out to be very important in the critically ill patient. There are two fundamental steps the body can take. It can increase cardiac output, or by extracting more oxygen from capillary blood, it can decrease $S\bar{v}O_2$.

When athletes exercise they can actually quintuple their cardiac output, increasing it from 5 l/min all the way up to 25 l/min. Most of us can at least triple our cardiac output.

On the other hand, if we look at oxygen extraction as in Figure 10, the normal $S\bar{v}O_2$ is 75% and the normal A-V saturation difference with an arterial saturation of 97% is 22%. When a normal individual is exercising $S\bar{v}O_2$ can decrease all the way down to 31%, thereby increasing A-V saturation difference from 22% to 66%. Once more, a factor of three.

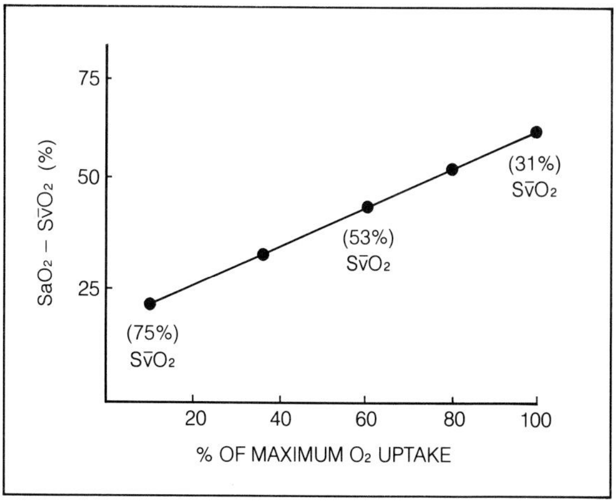

Figure 10

Normal individuals can increase their cardiac output by a factor of three and increase their A-V saturation difference by a factor of three. If you look at athletes and maximum oxygen consumption, by tripling cardiac output and by tripling the A-V saturation difference from 22% to 66%, an exercising man or woman can increase oxygen consumption by some nine-fold, as shown in Figure 11. Indeed, some athletes can do more.

MAXIMUM O_2 CONSUMPTION

$$C.O. \times Hb \times 13.8 \times (SaO_2 - S\bar{v}O_2)$$

$$15 \times 15 \times 13.8 \times (.97 - .31)$$

2049 ml/min

Figure 11

We are not here today to discuss what steps athletes take to increase their oxygen consumption. However, these same compensatory mechanisms are used by critically ill patients in Intensive Care Units.

Now, let us return to looking systematically at this expression of oxygen consumption, and go through the factors that can threaten the value of this expression.

First, a decrease in hemoglobin. I would hope that you would agree with me that there is no question if hemoglobin falls, that the value of this expression will decrease. Then, the body must take steps to compensate for the fall in hemoglobin to prevent consumption falling below the demand and to prevent the ominous development of lactic acidosis.

Patients with anemia have a high cardiac output as they attempt to keep consumption equal to demand. In fact, you can decrease hemoglobin from the normal of 15 gm/dl to 1.6 gm/dl; but if you triple cardiac output and you maximally desaturate venous blood, oxygen consumption will remain normal, as shown in Figure 12. That observation underlies the clinical axiom that you do not see lactic acidosis in uncomplicated anemia. Patients can compensate all the way down to a hemoglobin of 1.6 gm/dl. Clearly, patients with hemoglobins of 4, 5, and 6 will not develop lactic acidosis as long as nothing else is going on.

ANEMIA

$$C.O. \times Hb \times 13.8 \times (SaO_2 - S\bar{v}O_2)$$

$$15 \times 1.6 \times 13.8 \times (.97 - .31)$$

$$\dot{V}O_2 = 218 \text{ ml/min}$$

Figure 12

How about arterial saturation? There is no question that a fall in arterial saturation will threaten the value of this expression. There is no question that the body must take steps; and, in fact, it does. If someone's saturation falls all the way down from 97% to 38% (once again a remarkable fall in arterial saturation), and the patient triples cardiac output and maximally desaturates mixed capillary blood, oxygen consumption remains normal, as shown in Figure 13. This observation underlies the second clinical axiom: In uncomplicated arterial hypoxemia, you do not get lactic acidosis.

HYPOXEMIA

$$C.O. \times Hb \times 13.8 \times (SaO_2 - S\bar{v}O_2)$$

$$15 \times 15 \times 13.8 \times (.38 - .31)$$

$$\dot{V}O_2 = 217 \text{ ml/min}$$

Figure 13

We all have patients with chronic lung disease, who run PO_2 levels of 35 mmHg, with arterial oxygen saturations of 65% to 70%. They do not develop lactic acidosis unless something else is going on. Clearly, if the arterial PO_2 goes low enough, you can exhaust the compensatory mechanisms. But, by and large, do not expect to see lactic acidosis with the kinds of hypoxemia we see clinically. Or, perhaps expressed in a different way, if you do see lactic acidosis in someone with a PO_2 of 40 mmHg or 45 mmHg, you cannot explain it by the hypoxemia you are observing. Figure 14 demonstrates that. Two years ago a 70 year old man came in with respiratory failure. He had a chronic respiratory disease just at a point where the PO_2 is 19 and the lactate is normal. Hypoxemia alone does not cause lactic acidosis.

HYPOXEMIA ALONE DOES NOT CAUSE LACTIC ACIDOSIS	
70 Year Old Male With Respiratory Failure	
pH	= 7.29
pCO_2 (mmHg)	= 64
PO_2 (mmHg)	= 19
HCO_3 (mEq/l)	= 30
Lactate (mmol/l)	= 0.9

Figure 14

We have seen that the body has excellent compensatory mechanisms to cope with decreases in hemoglobin and arterial saturation. We are left with the final threat to oxygen consumption — a decrease in cardiac output. A decrease in cardiac output is qualitatively different than a decrease in hemoglobin or arterial saturation. Why? A fall in cardiac output not only threatens the value of this expression in the same way that anemia and arterial desaturation do, but it also eliminates one of the major compensatory mechanisms. Therefore, instead of being left with a nine-fold safety margin as you have with anemia or arterial desaturation, you are left with a three-fold safety margin. The only compensatory steps the body can take when cardiac output falls is to extract more oxygen and decrease $S\bar{v}O_2$.

Before thermodilution cardiac output was easily available in the ICU environment, $S\bar{v}O_2$ was called a "poor-man's cardiac output". When cardiac output decreased, $S\bar{v}O_2$ fell. Looking at that relationship the other way, if a decrease in $S\bar{v}O_2$ with a normal arterial saturation and hemoglobin was found, it meant cardiac output was low, as shown in Figure 15.

CAUSES OF ↓ $S\bar{v}O_2$

1. Anemia
2. Low Cardiac Output
3. Arterial Oxygen Desaturation
4. ↑ Oxygen Consumption

Figure 15

With anemia and arterial desaturation a normal person can tolerate a tremendous decrease in these values as compared to normal. However, once cardiac output has decreased to one-third of its normal value the one compensatory mechanism available has been exhausted, and lactic acidosis will occur. Perfusion failure probably remains the most common cause of lactic acidosis in a clinical setting.

CONTINUOUS MONITORING OF MIXED VENOUS OXYGEN SATURATION

3

THEORY APPLIED TO PRACTICE

John C. McMichan, M.B., B.S., Ph.D.*

Now that continuous monitoring of oxygen saturation in mixed venous blood ($S\bar{v}O_2$) is both feasible and accurate[1], it is necessary to review the interpretation and significance of changes in this variable. This can be achieved by applying the concepts of the oxyhemoglobin dissociation curve and the Fick Equation to a variety of clinical situations.

*Mayo Clinic
200 First Street SW
Rochester, Minnesota 55905

The oxyhemoglobin dissociation curve illustrated in Figure 1 demonstrates that under standard conditions of temperature, carbon dioxide tension, pH and hemoglobin concentration, a $S\bar{v}O_2$ of 75% is equivalent to an oxygen tension of 40 mmHg. When the blood is 100% saturated with oxygen, the content (CO_2) is 20 volumes %, while that in mixed venous blood is 15 volumes %. The difference between arterial and mixed venous oxygen content is, thus, 5 volumes %.

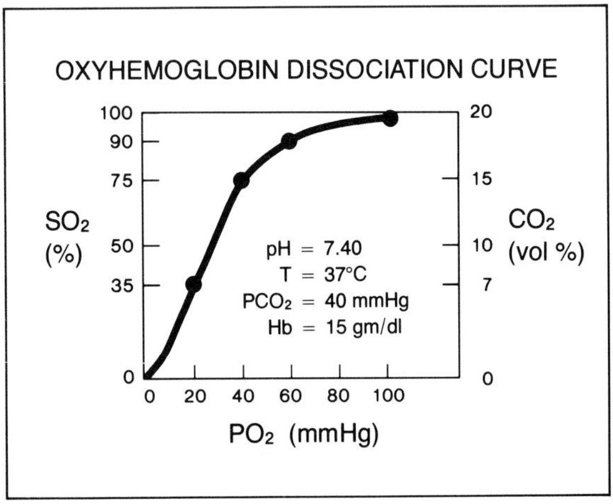

Figure 1

The Fick Equation is commonly used to derive cardiac output. However, when this equation is rearranged it can be shown that the mixed venous oxygen content depends proportionately on the arterial oxygen content and the cardiac output and inversely on the oxygen consumption.

$$\text{Venous } O_2 \text{ Content} = \text{Arterial } O_2 \text{ Content} - \frac{O_2 \text{ Consumption}}{\text{Cardiac Output}}$$

This same equation can be used to relate $S\bar{v}O_2$ to the arterial oxygen saturation, the oxygen consumption, cardiac output and hemoglobin concentration.

$$\begin{matrix}\text{Mixed Venous} \\ O_2 \text{ Saturation}\end{matrix} \approx \begin{matrix}\text{Arterial } O_2 \\ \text{Saturation}\end{matrix} - \frac{O_2 \text{ Consumption}}{\text{Cardiac Output} \times \text{Hb}}$$

It is the interplay between these four factors that results in the $S\bar{v}O_2$ measured by the fiberoptic pulmonary artery catheter. For this discussion, these factors are demonstrated on a series of oxyhemoglobin dissociation curves. Figure 2 shows both the arterial (open circle) and mixed venous (closed circle) points. The area of the square represents oxygen consumption ($\dot{V}O_2$) in ml/min, and is proportional to the product of cardiac output and the difference between arterial and mixed venous oxygen saturation; $\dot{V}O_2 \sim Q \cdot (SaO_2 - S\bar{v}O_2)$. Changes in the area of the square signify changes in oxygen consumption. Variation in the dimension of the sides of the square are related to changes in cardiac output and/or blood oxygen saturation.

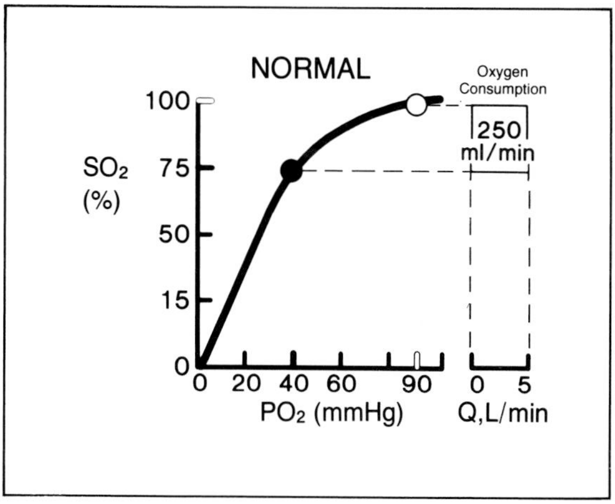

Figure 2

Oxygen saturation represents the amount of oxygen bound to hemoglobin, and this in turn accounts for about 98% of the oxygen carried in the blood, as shown in Figure 3. The remaining small proportion is due to oxygen physically dissolved in the plasma. These two amounts of oxygen when added together provide total oxygen content. However, it is important to notice that oxygen carriage by hemoglobin is far more important than oxygen carriage by plasma and, therefore, saturation is a more clinically significant entity than is tension.

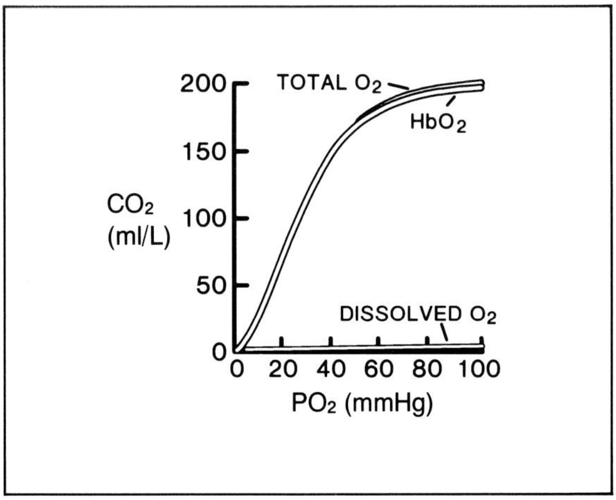

Figure 3

The arterial oxygen content is decreased, if the hemoglobin concentration is decreased. In the example shown in Figure 4 the hemoglobin concentration has been drastically reduced from 15.5 gm/100 ml to 3.9 gm/100 ml. If the arterial oxygen tension was 90 mmHg, arterial oxygen saturation could be normal, but arterial oxygen content would be reduced to about 50 ml/L of blood. If the usual arteriovenous oxygen content of 50 ml/L were to maintain in this example, there would be no oxygen left in the mixed venous blood. However, compensation has occurred. The cardiac output has increased to 8 L/min while the oxygen consumption has remained stable, and oxygen extraction by necessity has decreased to 31 ml/L. Under these circumstances the mixed venous oxygen content was only 19 ml/L, or about 10% saturated. Therefore, in this example, despite the cardiac compensation, the reduced level of hemoglobin and, therefore, of oxygen content produced a marked reduction in $S\bar{v}O_2$ to a level associated with permanent cellular damage.

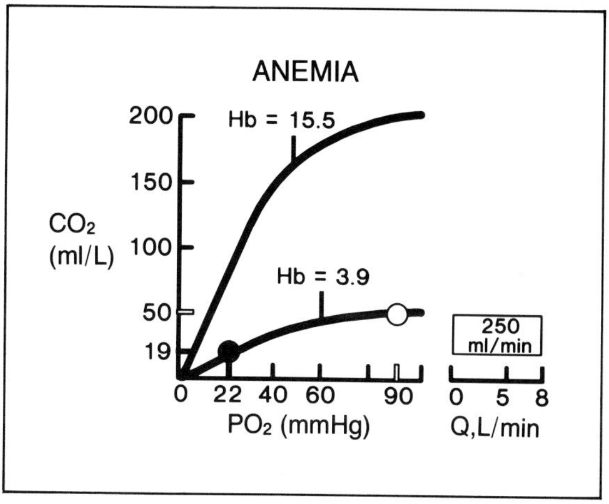

Figure 4

As already mentioned, the normal arteriovenous oxygen content difference is 50 ml/L of blood, as shown in Figure 5. If the amount of oxygen extracted during passage through the tissues is increased, the mixed venous oxygen content will fall.

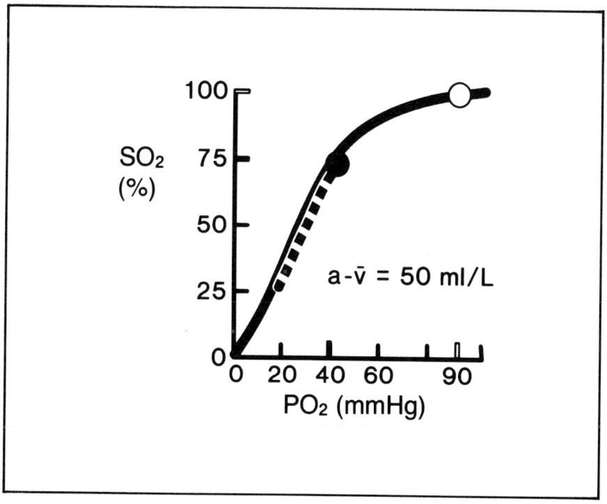

Figure 5

A level of $S\bar{v}O_2$ of 75% is usually quoted as the normal value. A range of 68-77% is acceptable, while increases above this level are relatively uncommon. Prominent among the causes for an increase in $S\bar{v}O_2$ is sepsis, and a progressively increasing $S\bar{v}O_2$ can be an early indication of decreased peripheral oxygen consumption and increased peripheral shunting due to sepsis. This left-to-right shunting of arterial blood in the periphery can also be found in conditions such as Paget's disease of the bone, cell poisoning (as in the cyanide toxicity associated with excessive use of nitroprusside[2]) and in those patients suffering from hypothermia.

However, probably the most common cause of an increase in $S\bar{v}O_2$ is a wedged pulmonary artery catheter. When the balloon at the end of the pulmonary artery catheter is inflated the blood distal to the balloon stagnates, absorbs oxygen from the surrounding ventilated alveoli and becomes closer in saturation to arterial blood.

A $S\bar{v}O_2$ of less than 60%, as shown in the table in Figure 6, usually represents cardiac decompensation leading progressively to lactic acidosis, the onset of unconsciousness and permanent cellular damage when the saturation is below 20%.

Mixed Venous Oxygen

Saturation (%)	Condition
77	Sepsis, L R shunt Excess inotrope Hypothermia Cell poisoning Wedged catheter
68-77	Normal range
75	Mode
60	Cardiac decompensation
53	Lactic acidosis
32	Unconsciousness
20	Permanent damage

Figure 6

By utilizing this information, each of the factors in the Fick Equation can be considered individually and observed for its effect on $S\bar{v}O_2$. However, it is important to point out that these factors are interrelated, and that a change in one is usually followed by a compensatory change in another to maintain the status quo. For the sake of clarity in this discussion, individual changes will be considered in the beginning.

If the oxygen uptake in the lung is deficient, the arterial oxygen saturation will fall. As suggested in the example in Figure 7, an arterial oxygen saturation of 75%, (equivalent to an arterial oxygen tension of 40 mmHg) in the presence of a normal arteriovenous oxygen content difference, a normal cardiac output and a normal oxygen consumption level will produce a decrease in $S\bar{v}O_2$ to about 50% (equivalent to an oxygen tension of 26 mmHg) Thus, decreased arterial oxygen saturation produced decreased $S\bar{v}O_2$.

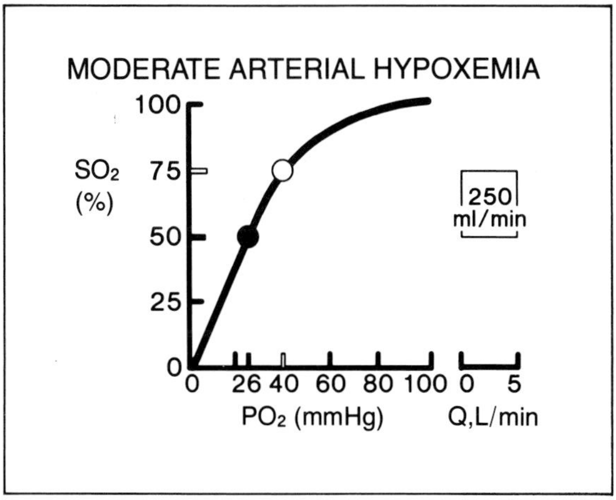

Figure 7

This mechanism is demonstrated in Figure 8, which is a recording of $S\bar{v}O_2$ of a patient who required mechanical ventilation. $S\bar{v}O_2$ was about 70% while the patient was receiving an inspired oxygen fraction of 0.6. When this fraction was decreased to 0.4 there was a decrease in $S\bar{v}O_2$ to 60%. The measured cardiac output in this patient did not change. Also of importance was the rapidity with which the change in $S\bar{v}O_2$ occurred. The response time of the oximeter system is very rapid.

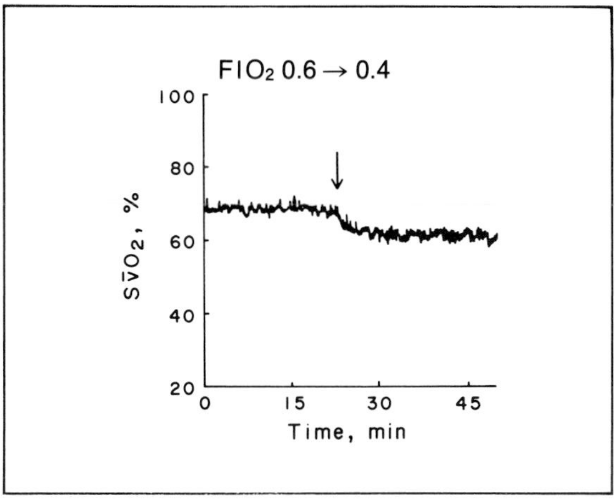

Figure 8

In the patient shown in Figure 9, who required mechanical ventilation and PEEP, $S\bar{v}O_2$ was reduced to about 52%. To obtain a measure of the pulmonary artery wedge pressure in this patient, the balloon at the end of the catheter was inflated and resulted in an increase of saturation, indicating successful wedging of the catheter. The mechanical ventilation and PEEP were then discontinued for 30 seconds to measure the wedge pressure, and a marked decrease in saturation occurred. Once the ventilator and PEEP were restored, a period of about 15 minutes was required before $S\bar{v}O_2$ again approached 60%. In this particular patient mechanical ventilation and PEEP should not have been discontinued, even for a very short time.

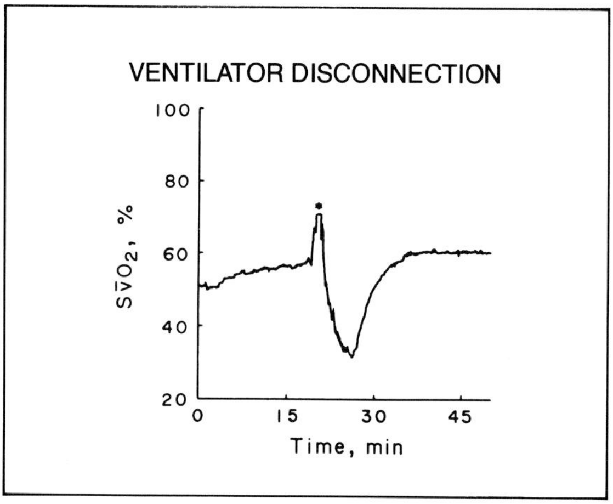

Figure 9

In another patient, depicted in Figure 10, who also required mechanical ventilation for the Adult Respiratory Distress Syndrome, the ventilator mode was changed from one of an assist/control to intermittent mandatory ventilation with a resultant rise in $S\bar{v}O_2$ which was maintained, indicating that the change in ventilator settings was appropriate for that patient at that particular time. Once again the alteration in $S\bar{v}O_2$ occurred rapidly, easily before any arterial blood gas analysis could be made to check correctness of the change of ventilator settings.

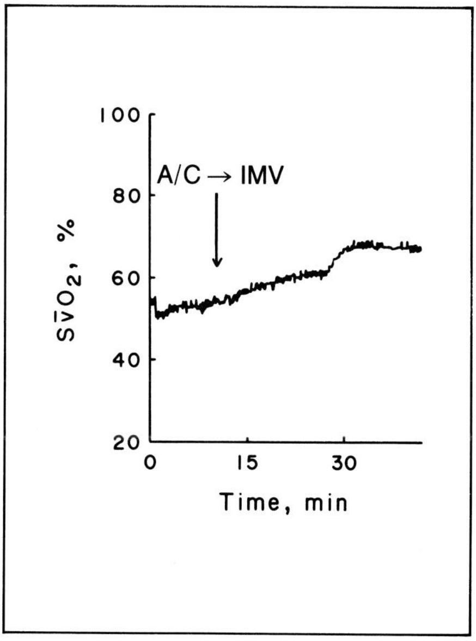

Figure 10

Another factor in the Fick Equation affecting $S\bar{v}O_2$ is the amount of oxygen consumed by the body as a whole. This is indicated by the value in the square in Figure 11, which demonstrates the changes that may occur in a patient under conditions of increased metabolism. The thyrotoxic patient provides such an example. The arterial oxygen saturation and tension were normal, but the oxygen consumption had increased to 560 ml/min. The cardiac output had also increased to 7.5 L/min. The height of the square is increased, indicating that the oxygen extraction had also increased in this example. As a result of these changes, $S\bar{v}O_2$ was approximately 63%.

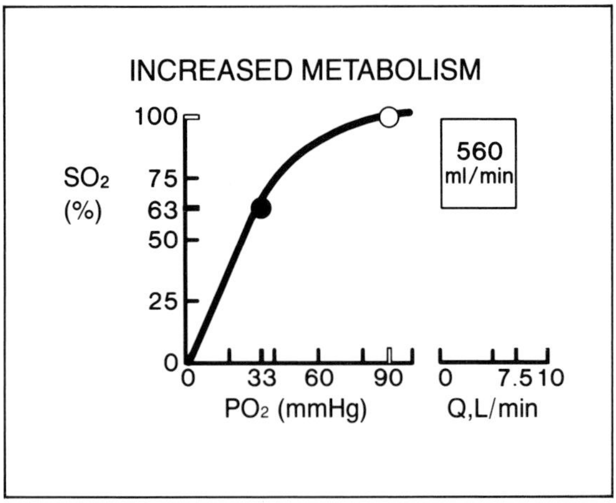

Figure 11

Another example of increased oxygen consumption is given by the exercising patient shown in Figure 12. Due to increases in respiratory function associated with exercise, the arterial blood oxygen content was maximized. Oxygen consumption ($\dot{V}O_2$) was greatly increased to 2 L/min. To accommodate these changes the cardiac output had also markedly increased to 16 L/min, but this was not adequate to supply tissue needs, and oxygen extraction increased. The result of these changes in oxygen consumption was a $S\bar{v}O_2$ of 40%. Thus, changes in oxygen consumption can be demonstrated by changes in $S\bar{v}O_2$.

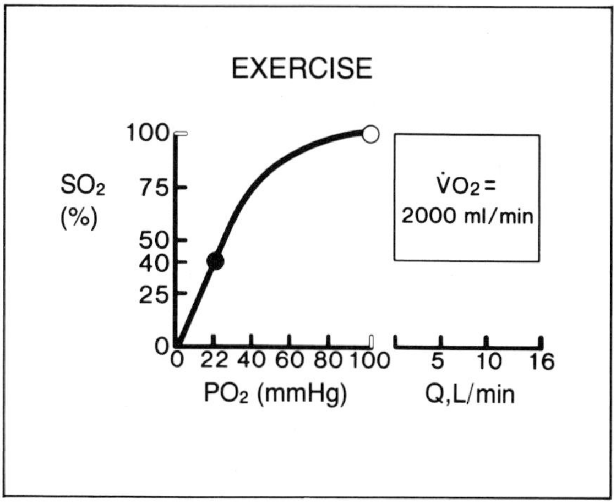

Figure 12

Patients receiving mechanical ventilation may become agitated and physically struggle against the activities of the ventilator. This represents exercise and is demonstrated by widely changing levels of $S\bar{v}O_2$, as seen in Figure 13. When the patient is adequately sedated these changes are markedly decreased.

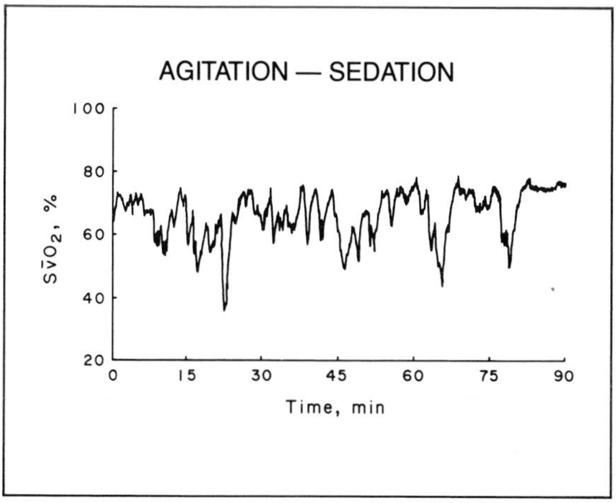

Figure 13

To a lesser extent, but nevertheless important, are the changes in $S\bar{v}O_2$ that come about very frequently as a result of simple and routine nursing maneuvers, as shown in Figure 14. In this example taken from a mechanically ventilated patient, $S\bar{v}O_2$ varied from 70% to 45% in association with bathing and turning the patient.

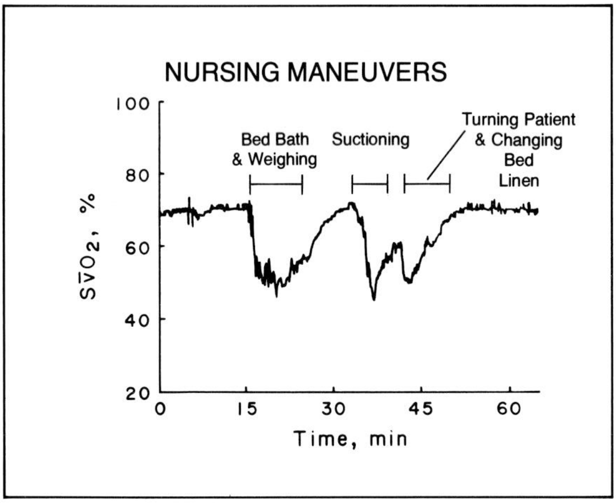

Figure 14

Before the advent of the pulmonary artery catheter with thermodilution capability, $S\bar{v}O_2$ was often used to interpret changes in cardiac output. This interpretation may well be correct if arterial oxygen saturation, peripheral oxygen utilization and left-to-right shunting of the blood remain constant. Some of these features are demonstrated on the oxyhemoglobin dissociation curve in Figure 15. With an arterial oxygen saturation of 100% in this example, oxygen consumption had not changed, but the cardiac output had fallen to 2 L/min. In order to provide adequate tissue oxygenation oxygen extraction had increased, and the resulting $S\bar{v}O_2$ was 38%. Thus, a decrease in cardiac output had produced a decrease in $S\bar{v}O_2$.

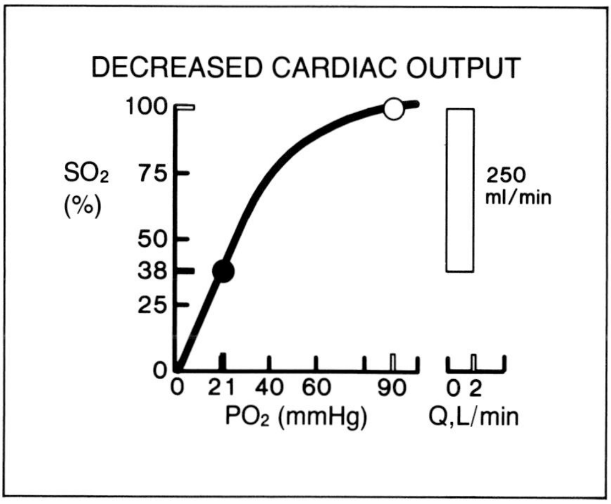

Figure 15

The effect of a low cardiac output upon the measurement of $S\bar{v}O_2$ in a patient with cardiogenic shock can be demonstrated. Such patients consistently show decreased $S\bar{v}O_2$, indicating that the low cardiac output necessitated an increase in oxygen extraction from the blood to provide tissue needs. A sudden decrease in $S\bar{v}O_2$ occurs at the time of cardiac arrest. Figure 16 illustrates two other important features: First, that $S\bar{v}O_2$ returned to the prearrest level with successful resuscitation, thus providing an indicator of the adequacy of resuscitation; and secondly, that there was a period of approximately 15 minutes before the arrest during which $S\bar{v}O_2$ gradually decreased, and during which an alert observer may have been able to prevent the subsequent arrest. As a result of this and other experiences, it is now recommended to routinely set the low limit alarm on the oximeter to about 60%.

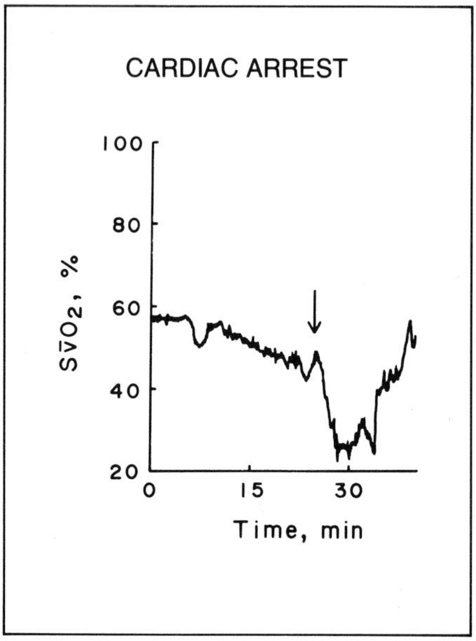

Figure 16

Cardiac output in the hypovolemic patient may be improved by crystalloid infusion. This was demonstrated in a patient, shown in Figure 17, in whom monitoring commenced soon after the completion of surgery for abdominal aortic aneurysm. The decrease in $S\bar{v}O_2$ was associated with systemic hypotension and a low pulmonary artery wedge pressure, which was measured frequently as indicated by the asterisk in the figure. At each of the points marked "a" a 100 ml bolus of crystalloid solution was infused during five minutes. Each bolus produced a transient rise in $S\bar{v}O_2$, indicating an improvement in preload to the heart. As each bolus improved both $S\bar{v}O_2$ and the wedge pressure a rapid and continuous infusion was started at "b", resulting in a return of $S\bar{v}O_2$ to a normal level. During this hour when postoperative hypovolemia was corrected, $S\bar{v}O_2$ monitoring provided valuable information on diagnosis of low cardiac output and the adequacy of its treatment. The same principle can be applied to the determination of the optimum dosage of cardiac inotropes and peripheral vasodilators.

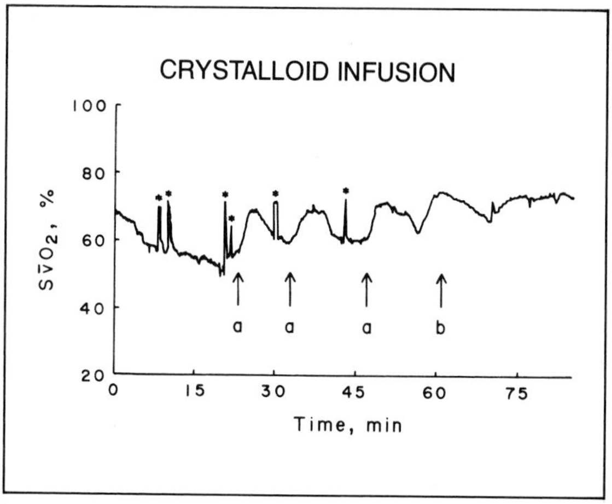

Figure 17

Continous monitoring of $S\bar{v}O_2$ is of particular value in the management of the patient with the Adult Respiratory Distress Syndrome (ARDS). In the example illustrated in Figure 18 oxygen consumption, cardiac output and oxygen extraction were all normal. However, arterial oxygen saturation was decreased due to the pulmonary disease. With standard oxygen extraction the $S\bar{v}O_2$ became 55%.

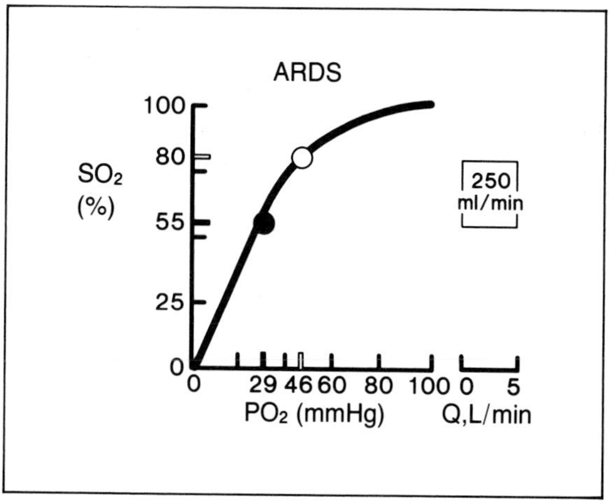

Figure 18

The addition of positive end-expiratory pressure (PEEP) to the ventilator mechanics is often used to try and reverse the deficit in arterial oxygen saturation. In Figure 19, which is similar to the previous one, the arterial oxygen saturation is 80%. PEEP was added, but it reduced the cardiac output as one of its side effects, in this case to 2.5 L/min. Oxygen consumption remained normal, but oxygen extraction increased. Thus, the addition of PEEP decreased $S\bar{v}O_2$ from the previous level of 55% to the equivalent of 30%, showing that PEEP under these circumstances was not indicated.

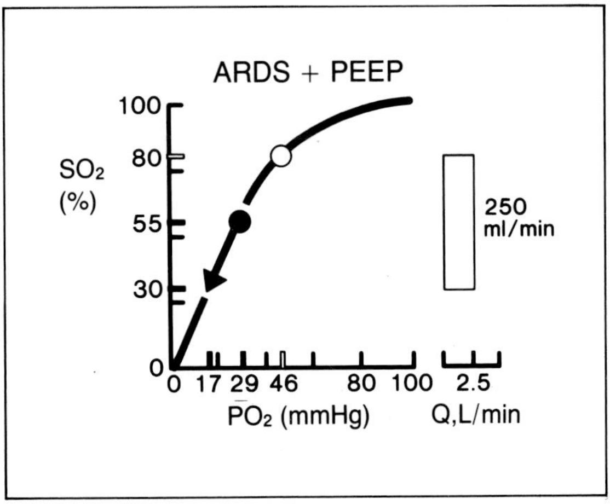

Figure 19

The beneficial effects of PEEP, however, can also be demonstrated. Figure 20 depicts a patient who was receiving 100% oxygen and who had an arterial oxygen tension of 50 mmHg. At the same time $S\bar{v}O_2$ was approximately 62%. PEEP was added to improve the arterial oxygen saturation and to allow a decrease to a nontoxic level of the amount of oxygen administered. There was little change when 5 cm H_2O PEEP was added to the ventilator circuitry. There was a small increase in saturation when 10 cm H_2O was added and an even more marked increase with 15 and 20 cm H_2O pressure. At the last level, $S\bar{v}O_2$ reached a plateau of 80%. A repeat of the arterial blood gas analysis showed that while the patient was still breathing 100% oxygen the arterial oxygen tension had risen markedly, permitting a decrease in the inspired oxygen fraction to the safe level of 0.5. This change produced a $S\bar{v}O_2$ of approximately 65% with an arterial oxygen tension of 160 mmHg. Thus, in this patient, PEEP of 20 cm H_2O permitted a decrease of administered oxygen to 50%, and these changes were accomplished in less than one hour. Without the continuous monitoring of $S\bar{v}O_2$, it would have been necessary to make repeated measurements of arterial blood gas analysis and cardiac output during a much longer period in order to achieve the same results. This approach to adjusting PEEP can be repeated as frequently as necessary to obtain the optimum level[3].

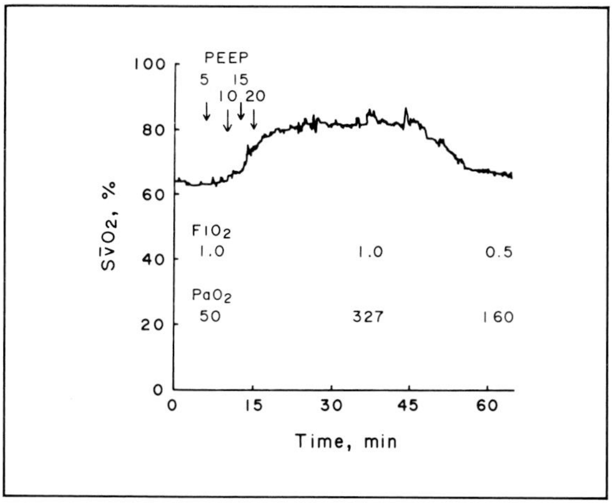

Figure 20

In summary, the continuous monitoring of $S\bar{v}O_2$ provides an understanding of the interrelationship between changes in cardiac and pulmonary function. Under most circumstances a fall in $S\bar{v}O_2$ indicates a worsening of cardiopulmonary function or an increase in peripheral oxygen consumption. Sepsis is a notable exception as its onset is indicated by a rise in saturation. Therapeutic maneuvers which return $S\bar{v}O_2$ towards the normal range do so as a result of improvement in cardiopulmonary function. Although $S\bar{v}O_2$ monitoring does not indicate which factor or combination of factors found in the Fick Equation have been affected, it does indicate that the particular maneuver is or is not appropriate, and it does this over a short space of time due to its rapid responsiveness.

In experience drawn from the use of about 200 fiberoptic catheters, the application of $S\bar{v}O_2$ monitoring has been of great benefit in many clinical situations. As the experience with the system increases, there is less guesswork in decision-making regarding adequacy of patient support and the appropriateness of a particular therapeutic modality in both the Operating Room and in the Intensive Care Unit.

REFERENCES

1. Baele P. L., McMichan J. C., Marsh H. M., Sill J. C., Southorn P. A.: Continuous monitoring of mixed venous oxygen saturation in critically ill patients. Anesth Analg 61:513-517, 1982.
2. Tinker J. H., Michenfelder J. D.: Cardiac cyanide toxicity induced by nitroprusside in the dog: potential for reversal. Anesthesiology 49:109-116, 1978.
3. Suter P. M., Fairlie H. B., Isenberg M. D.: Optimum end-expiratory airway pressure in patients with acute pulmonary failure. N Engl J Med 292:284-289, 1975.

CONTINUOUS $S\bar{v}O_2$ AS PREDICTOR OF CHANGES IN CARDIAC OUTPUT: CLINICAL OBSERVATIONS

4

John W. Hoyt, M.D.*
Frank D. Sottile, M.D.
Charles G. Durbin, M.D.
Robert F. Swain, B.S., R.R.T.
H. David McLachlan, B.S.

This presentation describes the use of pulmonary artery oximetry in postoperative cardiovascular surgery patients at the University of Virginia. The first goal is to look at mixed venous oxygen saturation ($S\bar{v}O_2$) as a predictor of changes in cardiac output, as documented by changes in thermodilution cardiac output. The second goal is to present brief clinical scenarios taken from tracings of mixed venous oximetry to further demonstrate events in the manipulation of the cardiovascular system, which were effectively tracked by $S\bar{v}O_2$.

The graph displayed in Figure 1 is a plot of cardiac output as calculated from $S\bar{v}O_2$, based on the Fick Formula. According to this formula, cardiac output is equal to oxygen consumption divided by arterial oxygen content minus mixed venous oxygen content times ten. In order to construct this particular graph, assumptions were made about oxygen consumption, saturation and hemoglobin. Dissolved oxygen was neglected and 100% arterial saturation was assumed. Following this, a series of calculations was established using various mixed venous saturations plugged into the Fick Equa-

*Box 238, Department of Anesthesiology
University of Virginia Medical Center
Charlottesville, VA 22908

tion to determine expected or predicted cardiac outputs at a particular $S\bar{v}O_2$. This is not a linear function, but rather a curvilinear function.

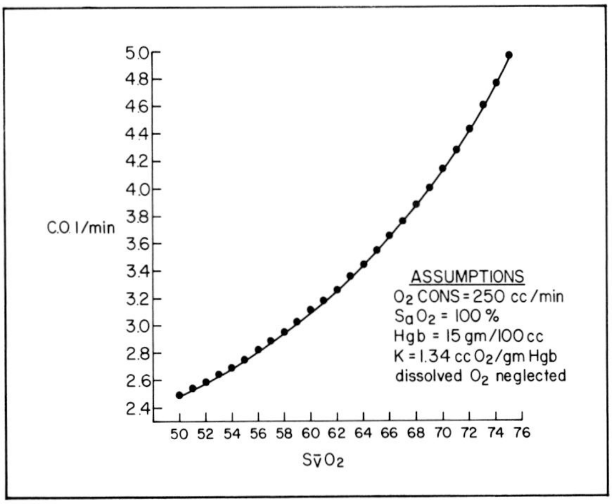

Figure 1

Relationship of $S\bar{v}O_2$ to cardiac output by Fick Formula:

$$C.O. = \frac{O_2 \text{ consumption}}{(CaO_2 - C\bar{v}O_2)\ 10}$$

Some of these assumptions can be changed, such as hemoglobin values (from 15 to 13), or oxygen consumption values (from 250 to 300, or even 500), as displayed in Figure 2. However, the shape of the curve stays basically the same, and all of these curves are parallel. It is possible to make some predictions about changes in cardiac output based on changes in $S\bar{v}O_2$ extracted from these curves.

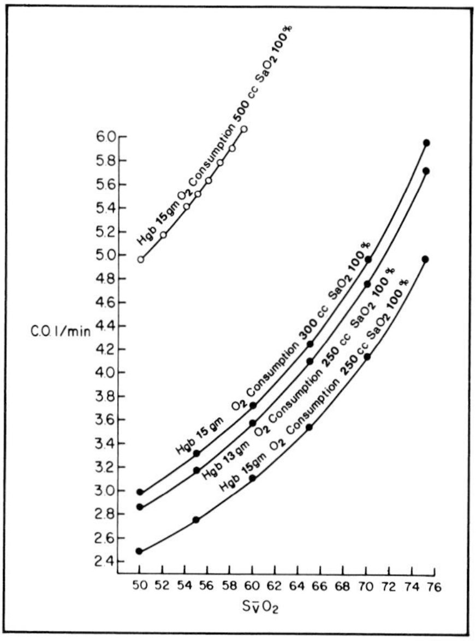

Figure 2

Effects of hemoglobin changes and oxygen consumption changes on the prediction of cardiac output from $S\bar{v}O_2$ — parallel curves.

Twelve thoracic and cardiovascular surgery patients at the University of Virginia were examined prospectively. Four of the patients were having valvular surgery and eight were having coronary artery bypass grafts.

The fiberoptic catheter was inserted preoperatively. $S\bar{v}O_2$ was continuously monitored for eight hours in the immediate postoperative period in the Surgical Intensive Care Unit. The following day (first postoperative day), starting at 8:00 a.m., $S\bar{v}O_2$ was monitored for another eight hours. With each hour's tracking of $S\bar{v}O_2$, thermodilution cardiac output was simultaneously measured and those values recorded on the $S\bar{v}O_2$ traces. Both arterial and mixed venous blood for oxygen saturation were drawn every two hours. The oxygen saturations were measured on an IL-282 Co-Oximeter to be certain that the measured saturations by co-oximetry were the same as those being recorded from the fiberoptic catheter.

Changes in pulmonary artery $S\bar{v}O_2$ noted on the bedside fiberoptic traces were utilized to predict changes in thermodilution cardiac output. These predictions were done from the Fick Cardiac Output Graph, seen in Figure 1. A measured change in pulmonary artery oxygen saturation from the previous hour was used to make a proportional adjustment in the last measured thermodilution cardiac output. Actual thermodilution cardiac output was then measured to compare actual changes for degree and direction of change to $S\bar{v}O_2$ predicted changes.

One might like to think that if measured thermodilution cardiac output was plotted against predicted cardiac output, there would be a perfect linear relationship, as shown in Figure 3.

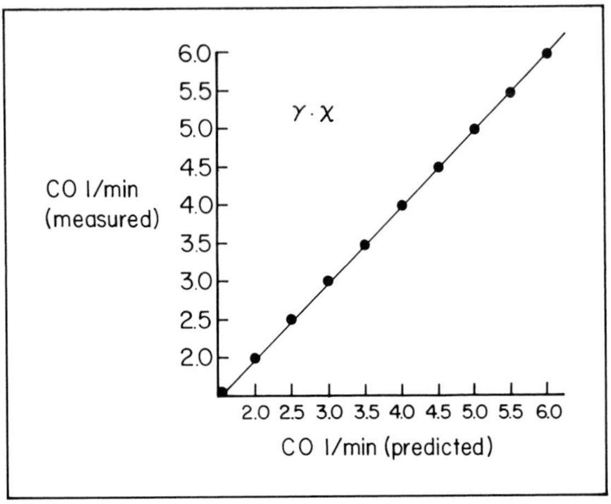

Figure 3

Calculation of a predicted cardiac output based on changes in $S\bar{v}O_2$, the known $S\bar{v}O_2$ - C.O. relationship from the Fick Principle, and the last measured thermodilution curve.

The actual relationship was good at times. It was less so during the operative day than during the first postoperative day. A total of 143 data points was gathered from 12 patients. Measured cardiac output was plotted against predicted changes in cardiac output in Figure 4. The result was a correlation coefficient of .60.

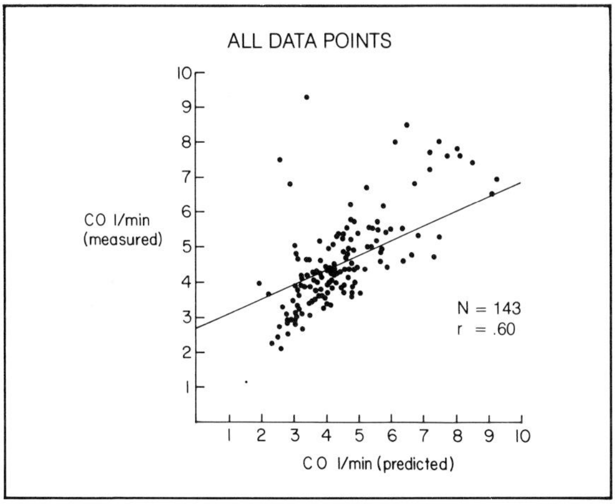

Figure 4
Relationship of measured thermodilution cardiac output to predicted cardiac output from S$\bar{v}O_2$ data in a group of postoperative cardiovascular surgery patients for the first 48 hours.

If the data was gathered only during the first postoperative day, as displayed in Figure 5, from 8:00 a.m. until 4:00 p.m., there were 63 data points. When measured thermodilution cardiac output was plotted against predicted cardiac output from S$\bar{v}O_2$ for the first postoperative day, a much better correlation of .85 was obtained.

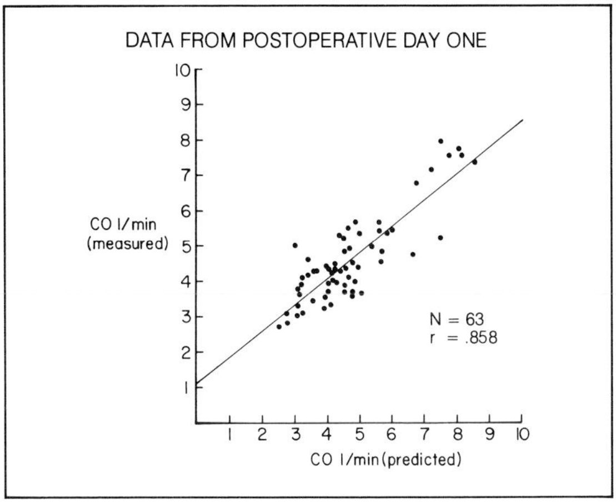

Figure 5
Relationship of measured thermodilution cardiac output to predicted cardiac output from S$\bar{v}O_2$ data in a group of cardiovascular surgery patients during postoperative day one.

The correlation on the first postoperative day was much better because of the tremendous amount of shivering which occurred in the immediate postoperative period. Postoperative cardiac surgery patients arrived in the Surgical Intensive Care Unit with body temperatures of about 34-35°C. Shivering during rewarming markedly increases oxygen consumption. It makes it more difficult to interpret a change in saturation and its relationship to cardiac output.

Some of the clinical scenarios seen during the study may be of interest. All of the figures are artist adaptions of actual traces acquired using the fiberoptic catheter. Shown are some of the different manipulations which are done with postoperative cardiovascular surgery patients.

The first scenario is the cardiovascular manipulation of unloading or afterload reduction using nitroprusside. The patient shown in Figure 6 had an $S\bar{v}O_2$ of 55%. This decreased to below 40%. A thermodilution cardiac output was done by a cardiovascular monitoring technician in the Surgical Intensive Care Unit. Because of a low cardiac output (2.1 l/min), the patient was started on nitroprusside at 0.5 mcg/kg/min. $S\bar{v}O_2$ increased to 55-60% and thermodilution cardiac output was measured the next hour. The increase in cardiac output was to a level of 3.23 l/min, which would have been predicted by the increase in $S\bar{v}O_2$.

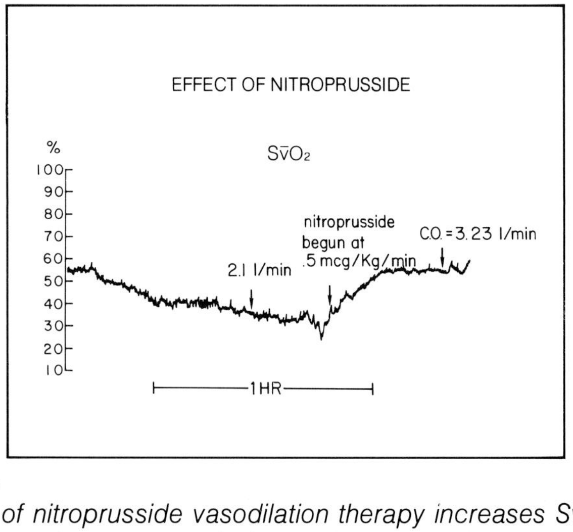

Figure 6
Initiation of nitroprusside vasodilation therapy increases $S\bar{v}O_2$ with simultaneous improvement in thermodilution cardiac output.

Another possibly less dramatic example is the patient depicted in Figure 7 whose starting saturation was 50%. Thermodilution cardiac output was 2.92 l/min. Sodium nitroprusside was started at 0.125 mcg/kg/min. The next thermodilution cardiac output was measured at 3.94 l/min. Measured $S\bar{v}O_2$ using the IL-282 Co-Oximeter was 58%. That was very consistent with changes noted from the fiberoptic pulmonary artery catheter.

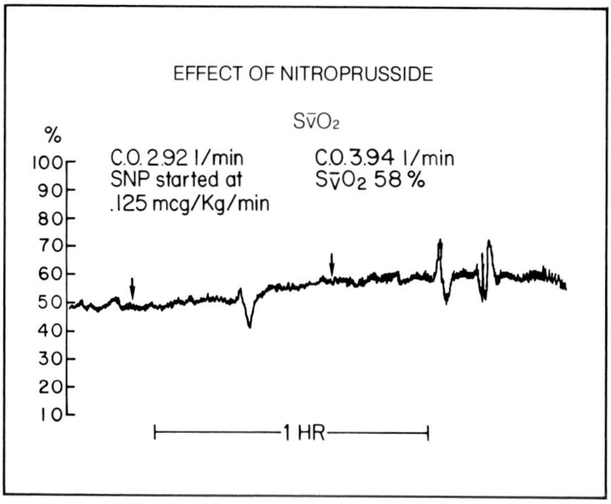

Figure 7
Slow improvement in $S\bar{v}O_2$ after nitroprusside started.

Next, in Figure 8, is an example of improving contractility in a postoperative cardiac surgery patient using isoproterenol (Isuprel®) as an inotrope. There is a starting saturation of 60%. $S\bar{v}O_2$ was 50% when the cardiovascular technician measured a thermodilution cardiac output of 2.95 l/min. The isoproterenol had been stopped a short time before. When the isoproterenol was restarted at 1 mcg/min and nitroprusside was decreased, $S\bar{v}O_2$ increased to about 70%. There was a concomitant increase in the thermodilution cardiac output.

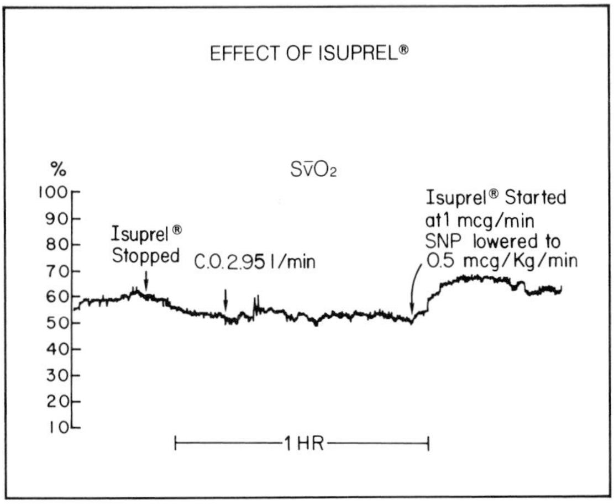

Figure 8
Improvement in $S\bar{v}O_2$ after inotropic support started with isoproterenol.

Generally, in the patients with manipulations of unloading and increases in inotropic function of the heart, we found a very good correlation between increases and decreases of $S\bar{v}O_2$ and changes in thermodilution cardiac output.

The greatest difficulty in interpreting a single selected saturation value was the role of oxygen consumption as related to shivering. The patient illustrated in Figure 9 had an output of 6.15 l/min. This would have given a calculated oxygen consumption of 187 ml/min, with an $S\bar{v}O_2$ of about 75%. Shivering commenced. As the patient began to rewarm, there was a drop in the $S\bar{v}O_2$ to 60%. When the cardiovascular technician measured thermodilution cardiac output it was actually 9.27 l/min, which was an increase from the previous value of 6.15 l/min, despite the decrease of $S\bar{v}O_2$. Oxygen consumption had increased to 458 ml/min. An increase in oxygen consumption had lowered the $S\bar{v}O_2$, rather than a decrease in cardiac output.

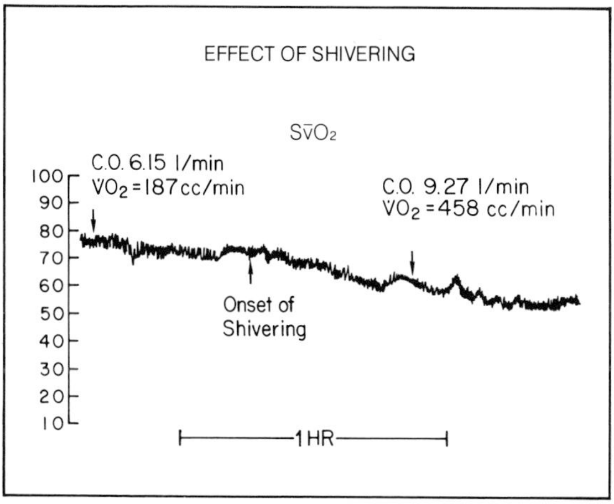

Figure 9
Marked effect of shivering and elevated oxygen consumption on $S\bar{v}O_2$, with an increase in thermodilution cardiac output as $S\bar{v}O_2$ falls.

An even more dramatic example of the effect of shivering is shown in Figure 10. Initial $S\bar{v}O_2$ was 55%, with a thermodilution cardiac output of 2.9 l/min. Shivering started 45 minutes later. Thermodilution cardiac output went up to 6.8 l/min. Oxygen consumption was 564 ml/min, with $S\bar{v}O_2$ in the 55-60% range. Because of the tremendous shivering, the patient was given a paralyzing dose of pancuronium (Pavulon®). After the shivering stopped, cardiac output fell to 5.6 l/min. There was a measured saturation of 76%, and oxygen consumption fell to 207 ml/min. Again, this is a good demonstration of how oxygen consumption affects saturation. If you limit oxygen consumption by eliminating shivering, this monitor becomes a much closer reflection of cardiovascular function.

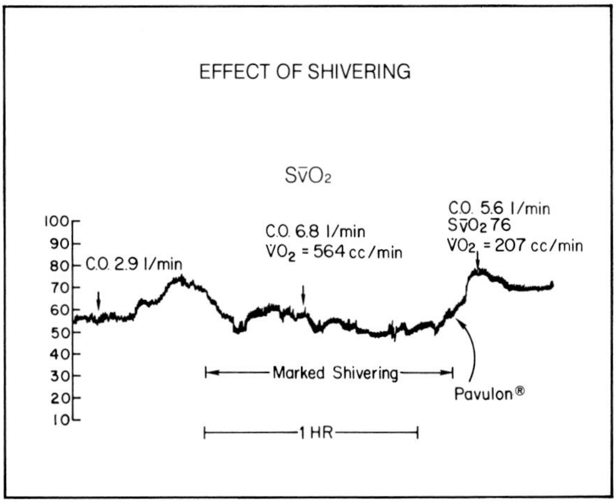

Figure 10

Further evidence of the prominent effect of shivering on $S\bar{v}O_2$. Note that when patient was paralyzed with pancuronium in order to stop the shivering, the $S\bar{v}O_2$ rose markedly as the thermodilution cardiac output fell.

There were several patients with whom we had difficulty in interpreting changes in saturation. These were labeled "noise" in Figure 11 because there was no other explanation for the changes. It appears that, clinically, these brief changes of only a minute's duration are really not very significant. It is necessary to see changes that go on for 10, 15, or 20 minutes before one can really rely on the fact that changes in cardiac output or oxygen consumption are reflected. There were several patients with these brief, repeated changes for which there was no explanation.

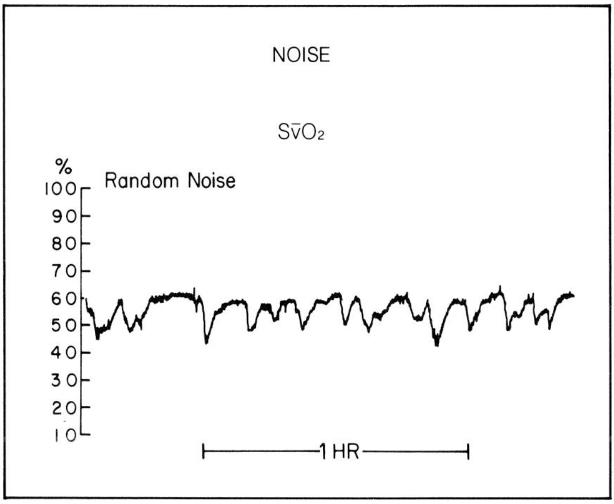

Figure 11
Baseline changes in S$\bar{v}O_2$ with no physiologic etiology.

In general, changes in saturation of less than 5% that are not sustained do not reliably reflect a change in cardiac output. On the other hand, changes of 5-10% that are sustained for 15 minutes are a valuable clinical guide to cardiac output and oxygen consumption.

The patient illustrated in Figure 12 had diarrhea in the postoperative state and got out of bed to use the bedside commode. The result was a drop in $S\bar{v}O_2$. At one particular time we did draw mixed venous blood and measured it on the IL-282 Co-Oximeter. There was a concomitant drop in *in vitro* $S\bar{v}O_2$ which was not just a function of the PA catheter coming against the wall of a vessel. When the patient got up and back into bed there was again a very brief, but not sustained, drop in saturation which was not correlated with changes in cardiac output.

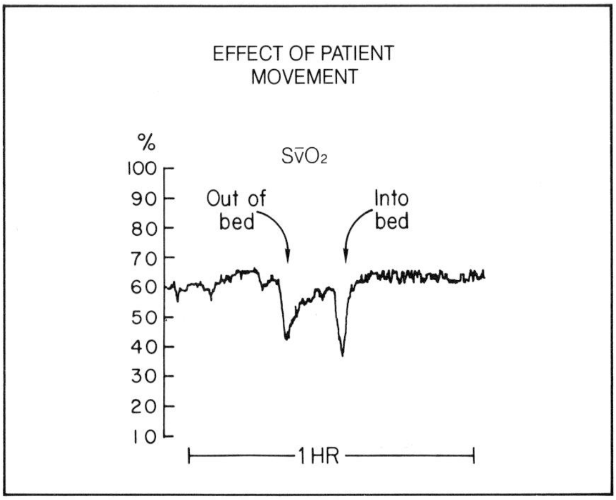

Figure 12
Changes in $S\bar{v}O_2$ with patient movement.

Several valuable clinical aids were obtained from this monitor in addition to trending cardiac output. The monitor was a very good way of detecting permanently wedged catheters. In the patient depicted in Figure 13, $S\bar{v}O_2$ was 50%. Suddenly, it rose to 70%, and then 75%. When the nurse looked at the oscilloscope, the catheter was in a permanently wedged position based on the waveform. When the catheter was brought back into a larger vessel one could see the drop in saturation.

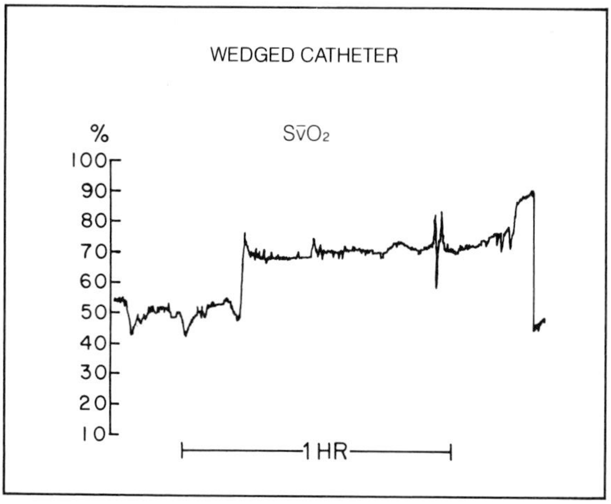

Figure 13
When the pulmonary artery catheter becomes permanently wedged, the $S\bar{v}O_2$ rises markedly as the oximeter begins to measure pulmonary capillary blood.

Figure 14 shows a patient who was being weighed in the Surgical Intensive Care Unit, and the attendant and nurse were having problems with the endotracheal tube. It was noted that the saturations dropped down to the 30% range.

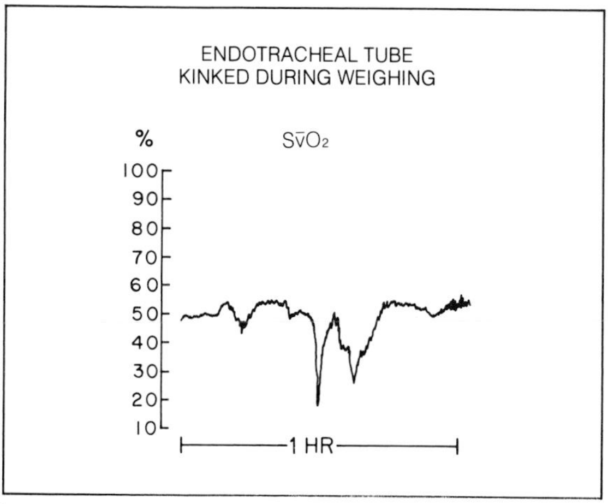

Figure 14
Detection of respiratory support malfunction by marked falls in $S\bar{v}O_2$.

In summary, continuous fiberoptic pulmonary artery oximetry is a very helpful clinical monitor in a trended form for patients with fluctuating cardiovascular performance. A single isolated value out of context of other clinical information is probably not very helpful. However, when a $S\bar{v}O_2$ is interpreted in light of a thermodilution cardiovascular profile and then trended as one manipulates the cardiovascular system with unloading or inotropes, or positive respiratory pressure, it becomes a very helpful tool in trending changes in cardiac output. It is a valuable tool, providing the patient does not have rapidly fluctuating oxygen consumption.

CONTINUOUS MEASUREMENT OF CORONARY SINUS OXYGEN SATURATION AS A METHOD FOR DETECTING CORONARY ARTERY DISEASE

5

Philip A. Poole-Wilson, M.D., M.R.C.P.*
Rudolph Canepa-Anson, M.D.

INTRODUCTION

We have investigated the use of a fiberoptic pulmonary artery catheter (Model P7110 Opticath®, Oximetrix, Inc.) for the continuous measurement of oxygen saturation. The device has been used in an attempt to resolve problems in the management of patients with heart failure and in the diagnosis of coronary artery disease. Records have been obtained with the catheter placed in the pulmonary artery, femoral vein and coronary sinus. Part of this work has been published as an abstract (Poole-Wilson et al, 1982).

EVALUATION OF EQUIPMENT

Initial studies were undertaken to assess the accuracy and drift of the catheter over a prolonged period. Values for the oxygen saturation in the pulmonary artery ($S\bar{v}O_2$) were compared with values obtained by measurement on a withdrawn sample of blood using a standard benchtop oximeter (American Optical). Thirty-one comparisons were made in 15 patients. The oxygen saturation ranged

*Cardiothoracic Institute and National Heart Hospital,
2 Beaumont Street, London, W1N 2DX

from 38% to 82%. The correlation coefficient was 0.96 and the slope of the relationship was not different from the anticipated line of identity.

A similar comparison was made with the catheter placed in the coronary sinus over a range of oxygen saturation from 25% to 40%. The correlation coefficient was 0.87, and the slope was, again, no different from the line of identity.

Catheters were left in the pulmonary artery for up to 72 hours. Drift was not a problem. Recalibration of the catheter once inserted was rarely necessary, but could easily be accomplished by withdrawal of a blood sample. A typical trace obtained over 12 hours is shown in Figure 1.

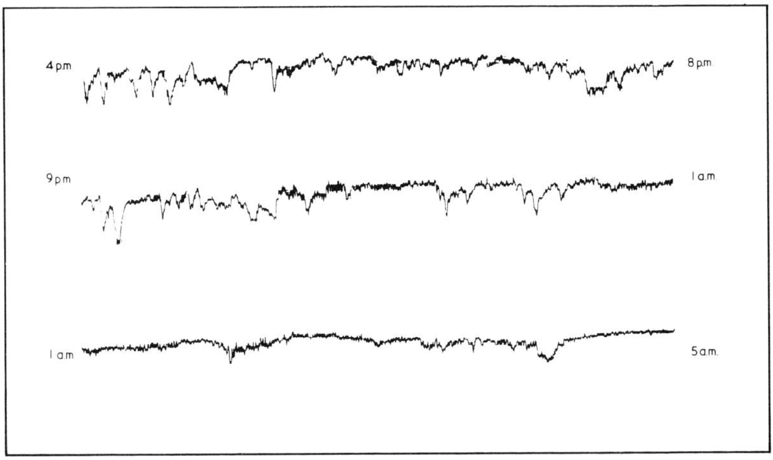

Figure 1

Continuous record of $S\bar{v}O_2$ of a patient with severe chronic heart failure.

CHRONIC HEART FAILURE

The availability of many new drugs (either positive inotropic agents or vasodilators) for the treatment of heart failure has given impetus to research concerned with understanding the fundamental physiology and the identification of patients who might benefit from a particular form of drug therapy.

If oxygen consumption and arterial oxygen saturation remain constant, then by the Fick Principle, $S\bar{v}O_2$ is related to cardiac output. If oxygen consumption increases and the cardiac output does not increase concurrently, $S\bar{v}O_2$ will fall.

A typical trace obtained from a patient with severe heart failure is shown in Figure 1.

$S\bar{v}O_2$ at rest is low, being approximately 60%. The trace during the evening shows many short periods when the saturation falls as low as 34%. These reductions are due to physical activity on the part of the patient and are characteristic of severe heart failure. An example on a faster time scale is shown in Figure 2.

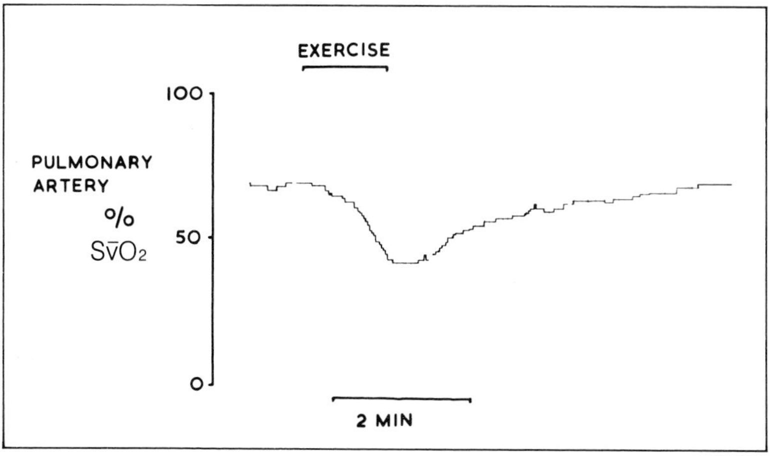

Figure 2

A continuous record of the effect of exercise on $S\bar{v}O_2$ in a patient with heart failure.

During the night the transient reductions in $S\bar{v}O_2$ are absent because the patient shown in Figure 1 is asleep, and the resting $S\bar{v}O_2$ is much higher (80%) than the value during the early evening (60%).

Patients with severe heart failure are usually limited either by breathlessness or by fatigue. With the use of powerful diuretics, fatigue, the causation of which is less well understood than shortness of breath, is becoming a more common limiting symptom. Fatigue appears to be associated with desaturation of venous blood from working skeletal muscle and the onset of anaerobic metabolism.

If a particular level of exercise is associated with a constant blood pressure and constant oxygen consumption by the limbs, then the effect of a drug intervention on blood flow to the limb can be assessed by measurement of the $S\bar{v}O_2$. A catheter can be inserted into the inferior vena cava or femoral vein. Direct and continuous recordings of the $S\bar{v}O_2$ can be obtained during an exercise test. Such a technique does not distinguish between increased nutrient blood flow to the limbs and increased blood flow through arterio-venous shunts.

CORONARY ARTERY DISEASE

Visualization of coronary arteries by angiography reveals anatomical obstructions. Whether such lesions are a cause, directly or indirectly, of ischaemia in the myocardium can only be demonstrated by the presence of symptoms, physical signs, exercise electrocardiography and some radioisotope techniques. All such methods are fallible.

The possibility exists that measurement of the oxygen saturation in the coronary sinus or coronary vein during some form of myocardial stress might be a sensitive indicator of reduced coronary flow, e.g. myocardial ischaemia (Chierchia et al, 1980). A catheter tip pH electrode has previously been used for this purpose (Cobbe and Poole-Wilson, 1982).

Recordings have been obtained from 16 patients who were undergoing cardiac catherization for the investigation of chest pain. Two patients had normal coronary arteries while the remainder had various degrees of coronary obstruction. Coronary angiography was performed by the Sones technique from the right arm. The Oximetrix, Inc. catheter was inserted into the left brachial vein and passed down the superior vena cava into the coronary sinus. The catheter can be manipulated and its shape is such that it passes easily into the coronary sinus. The position of the catheter was confirmed by injection of dye down the lumen of the catheter. An arterial pacing test was then undertaken. The heart rate was increased by ten beats per minute every minute (Cobbe and Poole-Wilson, 1982). The electrocardiogram and left ventricular or aortic pressure were recorded during the last ten seconds of each minute, when the pacemaker was turned off and the heart reverted to sinus rhythm.

The record in Figure 3 shows a typical trace in a patient who had no electrocardiographic changes during the pacing test.

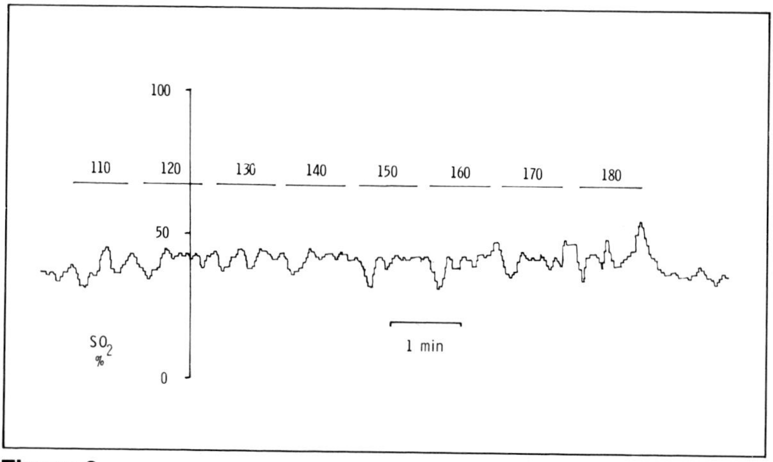

Figure 3
Oxygen saturation in the coronary sinus during an atrial pacing test of a patient who had no evidence of myocardial ischaemia.

The average value for the coronary sinus oxygen saturation remained constant so that the increased oxygen consumption of the heart was exactly accounted for by increase in coronary blood flow. At the higher heart rates it is evident that when pacing is initiated the coronary sinus oxyen saturation does fall, but returns to the control value within about 20 seconds. The coronary blood flow is being regulated by the metabolic requirements of the heart. Such rapid adjustments to increased myocardial oxygen consumption were anticipated since in the dog reactive hyperemia can be demonstrated after occlusion of coronary arteries for less than one second (Schwartz et al, 1982).

In patients with coronary artery disease in whom chest pain and/or electrocardiographic changes were evident, a different response was observed. A typical trace is shown in Figure 4.

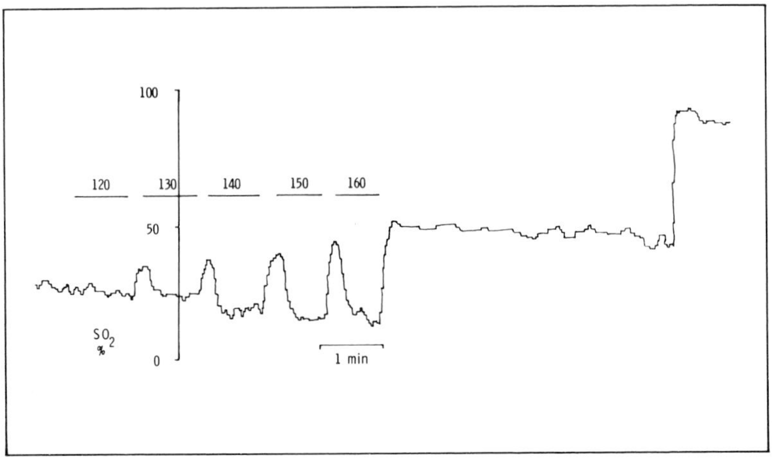

Figure 4
Oxygen saturation in the coronary sinus during an atrial pacing test of a patient who had electrocardiographic evidence of myocardial ischaemia developing during the test.

After an increment in heart rate the oxygen saturation fell and did not return to control values in the next 20 seconds, presumably because metabolic regulation of blood flow at the arterioles could not overcome the effect of stenoses in large coronary arteries. The oxygen saturation increased abruptly when pacing was terminated. Increasing heart rates were associated with lower values of saturation. Changes in oxygen saturation preceded changes in the electrocardiogram.

The records (Figures 3 and 4) from patients with and without myocardial ischaemia are sufficiently different to suggest that the technique might form a useful test for ischaemia of heart muscle, whatever its cause. Similar results have been reported in spontaneous angina, due not to fixed obstruction of coronary arteries, but to vasoconstriction (Chierchia et al, 1980).

The principal drawback to the method is that it is invasive and is unlikely to be useful in the detection of ischaemia in the inferior portion of the heart where blood drains into the coronary sinus close to its opening into the right atria. The potential advantage of the technique is that it is relatively simple and may provide a sensitive and highly specific metabolic indicator of myocardial ischaemia.

REFERENCES

1. Chierchia S., Brunelli C., Simonetti I., Lazzari M., Maseri A.: Sequence of events in angina at rest: primary reduction in coronary flow. Circulation 61: 759-768, 1980.
2. Cobbe S.M., Poole-Wilson P.A.: Continuous coronary sinus and arterial pH monitoring during pacing-induced ischaemia in coronary artery disease. British Heart Journal 47:369-374, 1982.
3. Poole-Wilson P.A., Canepa-Anson R., Langley G., Montgomery R.: Continuous recording of coronary sinus oxygen saturation during pacing test as a method for detection of coronary artery disease in patients with chest pain. British Heart Journal 47:204, 1982.
4. Schwartz G.G., McHale P.A., Greenfield J.C.: Hyperemic response of the coronary circulation to brief diastolic occlusion in the conscious dog. Circulation Research 50:28-37, 1982.

CONTINUOUS $S\bar{v}O_2$ AND OTHER NEW HEMODYNAMIC PARAMETERS AS EARLY INDICATORS OF HYPOVOLEMIA

6

Curtis A. Sheldon, M.D.*
Arnold S. Leonard, M.D., Ph.D.

The subject of our presentation is mixed venous oxygen saturation ($S\bar{v}O_2$) and other indicators of peripheral perfusion, and how these can be used for the assessment of volume status. Our laboratory has been interested in developing techniques of hemodynamic monitoring which accurately reflect volume changes intraoperatively. Our clinical experience has revealed that modalities for assessment of operative volume loss and replacement, in current use, are considerably less than optimal. Of course, such parameters would have to be safe and minimally invasive and, thereby, applicable for routine use. These considerations have led us toward developing methods of measuring the adequacy of peripheral perfusion.

We would like to present our experimental experience with some of these modalities. Our basic protocol, as shown in Figure 1, consists of a dog model with an anesthetic regimen similar to one in common clinical use. The animals are maintained on intermittent positive pressure ventilation with the tidal volume and respiratory rate adjusted such that normal arterial blood gases are documented prior to each study. Instrumentation includes catheters for mea-

*Department of Surgery
University of Minnesota Hospitals
Minneapolis, Minnesota 55455

surement of central venous pressure (CVP), peripheral postcapillary venous pressure (PCVP), central aortic pressure (AP), and an Oximetrix pulmonary artery catheter, which allows us to measure the pulmonary artery pressure (PAP), wedge pressure (PWP), cardiac output (CO), and mixed venous oxygen saturation ($S\bar{v}O_2$). Oximetrix catheters are similarly employed to measure central venous oxygen saturation ($CVSO_2$) and peripheral venous oxygen saturation ($PVSO_2$). Cannulation of the contralateral femoral artery and vein allows us to induce either controlled hemorrhage or plasma expansion.

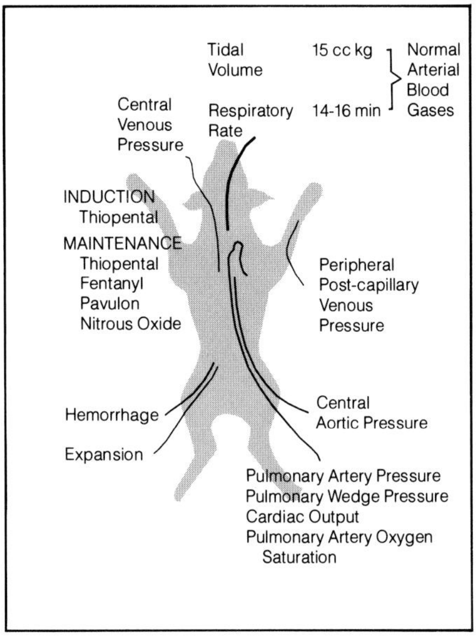

Figure 1
Anesthetic regimen and instrumentation for hemodynamic study.

The catheter which we have developed for the measurement of post-capillary venous pressure (PCVP) is a twenty-gauge polymeric double lumen catheter with a small balloon located approximately 1.5 cm from the tip of the catheter, and is manufactured by the Norton Company.

The catheter is advanced into a cutaneous vein of the forearm and threaded in a retrograde fashion such that the tip of the catheter lies within the forepaw, as illustrated in Figure 2.

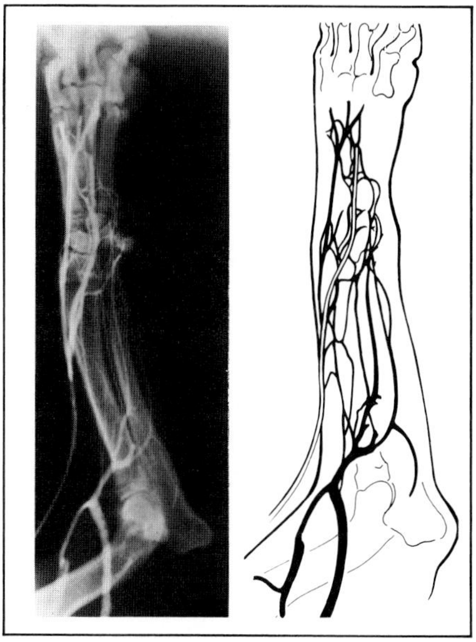

Figure 2

Venography demonstrates position of PCVP catheter. Note unoccluded venous collateral flow.

That the presence of the catheter itself does not alter venous flow is suggested by the fact that injection of contrast material rapidly fills multiple collaterals, and follow-up films show a very fast washout phase, as well.

The following graphs will demonstrate the response of the various parameters which we have evaluated to slow continuous hemorrhage. Eleven animals, using balanced anesthesia, were hemorrhaged at a rate of .65 cc/kg/min. The data was expressed as mean ± standard error of the mean. The parameters, expressed here as percent of baseline, were plotted against the estimated blood loss, expressed as percent of estimated blood volume. Statistical analysis was performed by a two-tailed T-test.

One of our investigational parameters, peripheral postcapillary venous pressure (an indicator of peripheral perfusion), fell in a very sensitive way during the early phases of surgically induced hemorrhage and continued to do so over the entire range of hemorrhage studied. In contrast, as we have learned to expect clinically, the arterial pressure and central venous pressure are relatively well maintained due to compensatory mechanisms until approximately

20-30% of the estimated blood volume has been extracted. Only then do they begin to fall in a meaningful way, as shown in Figure 3.

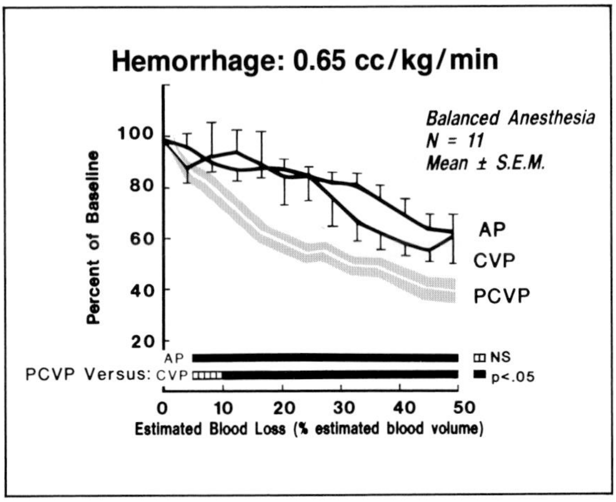

Figure 3
Response of AP, CVP, and PCVP to slow continuous hemorrhage.

There was a statistically significant difference between PCVP and these other two parameters over the entire range of hemorrhage studied. Central venous pressure and arterial pressure are the most commonly employed pressure parameters in current use for clinical monitoring.

Pulmonary artery pressure and pulmonary wedge pressure had responses similar to PCVP, as shown in Figure 4, in that they had a very nice linear drop which was, therefore, predictive of the actual depth of hemorrhage. There was only a minimal statistically significant difference between these two parameters and PCVP. There was a suggestion that PCVP was slightly more sensitive as an indicator of peripheral perfusion than were the central pressure parameters.

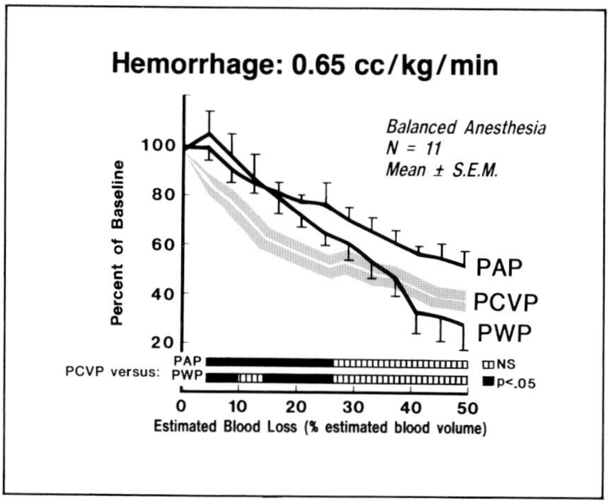

Figure 4

Response of PAP, PCVP, PWP to slow continuous hemorrhage.

Similarly, cardiac output and mixed venous oxygen saturation ($S\bar{v}O_2$) fell in a predictable and linear fashion, as shown in Figure 5. They are very closely correlated with the values that we obtained for PCVP, as we would expect since they are all, in essence, indicators of the adequacy of peripheral perfusion.

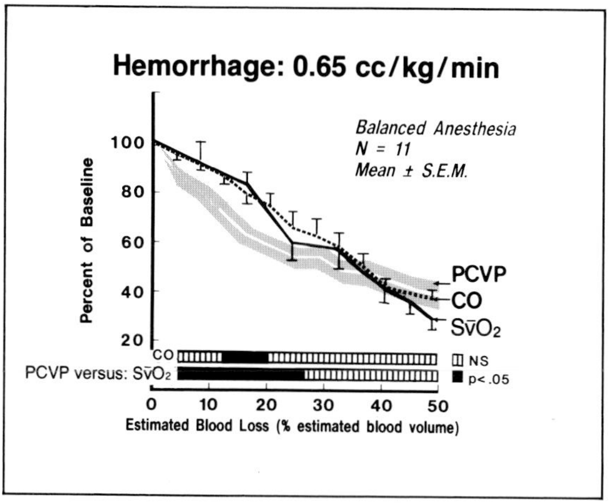

Figure 5

Response of PCVP, CV, $S\bar{v}O_2$ to slow continuous hemorrhage.

Equally important to the trend of the means is the reliability with which each of these parameters can reflect the depth of hemorrhage in each individual animal. This was determined by plotting the r-values, obtained by linear regression analysis, for each parameter against the depth of hemorrhage in each individual study. We have taken r-values of 0.8 or greater as having reliably predictive significance as to the depth of hemorrhage. As you can see in Figure 6, PCVP, pulmonary artery pressure, wedge pressure and cardiac output were all very well correlated with the actual extent of hemorrhage and, thereby, have a linear relationship. The central venous pressure, arterial pressure, and heart rate, as we have learned to expect, were very poor indicators of the actual depth of hemorrhage — either being insensitive or nonspecific. The $S\bar{v}O_2$ had a distribution that was exactly analogous to that encountered for cardiac output, so that it also was very predictive.

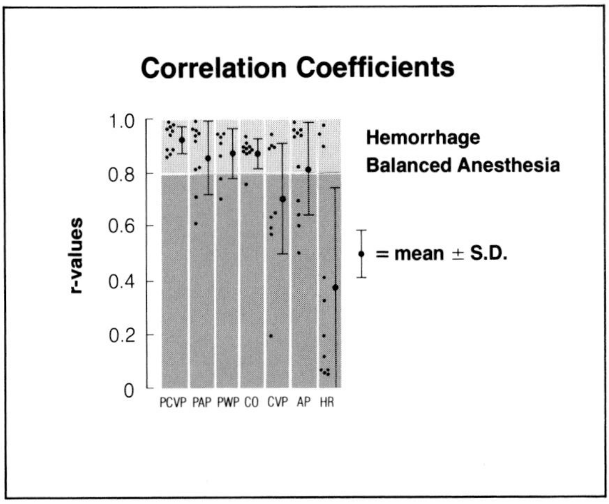

Figure 6

Predictive ability of various parameters in determining extent of hemorrhage.

Similarly, looking at plasma expansion in this way, as shown in Figure 7, we found that PCVP, the pulmonary pressures, the cardiac output, and CVP were all linearly predictive of the extent of plasma overexpansion (plasma expansion of normovolemic animals). Arterial pressure and heart rate were less than adequately predictive. Of course, one would not expect the $S\bar{v}O_2$ in this case to adequately predict the extent of overhydration, and it did not.

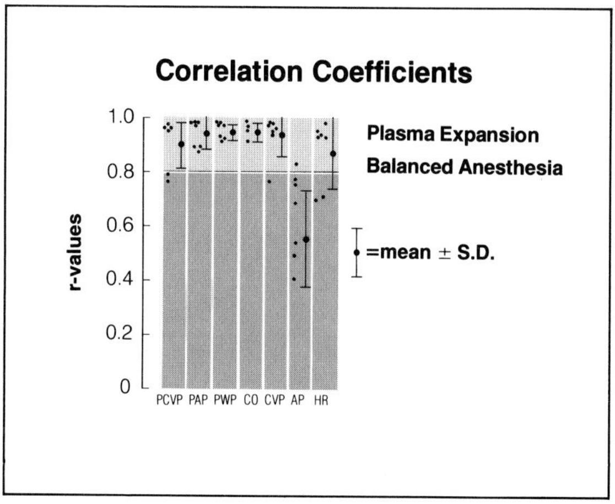

Figure 7
Predictive ability of various parameters in determining extent of plasma expansion.

There seems to be a very close relationship between the indicators of peripheral perfusion such as PCVP and cardiac output. When we pooled all of our data and plotted PCVP (expressed as percent of baseline) against cardiac output (expressed as percent of baseline), as displayed in Figure 8, we did find a very tightly correlated relationship. Linear regression analysis revealed an r-value of 0.96.

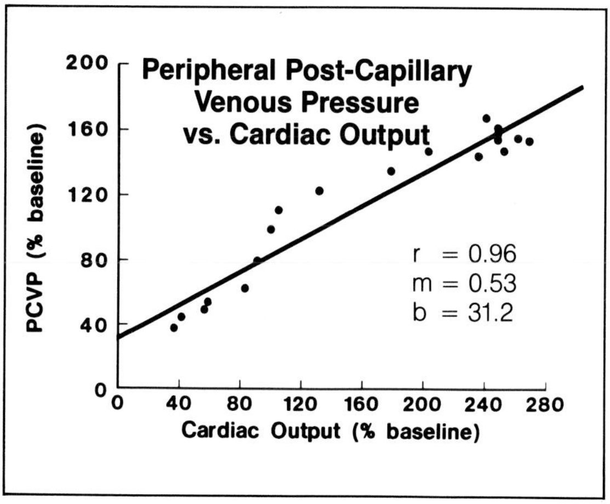

Figure 8
Correlation of PCVP and cardiac output.

We then directed our attention to more closely defining the relationship between cardiac output and PCVP (an example of an indicator of peripheral perfusion). To do this we looked at controlled venous return with an open-chest model, as pictured in Figure 9. The superior and inferior vena cava were cannulated and the azygous vein occluded, such that the entire venous return was brought into a reservoir. The blood from the reservoir was then brought through a cardiac bypass pump and placed directly back into the right atrium. In this way, by adjusting the rate of the cardiac bypass pump, we could selectively choose the venous return. In so doing, we were able to maintain anatomical continuity between the four chambers of the heart. We continuously monitored the caval pressure and measured the cardiac output by means of thermodilution (injection into the left atrium and thermistor located in the aortic arch). By adjusting the rate of the bypass pump, hence the rate of venous return, we could alter the cardiac output and look at the relationship between PCVP and cardiac output, with central venous pressure and intravascular volume held constant.

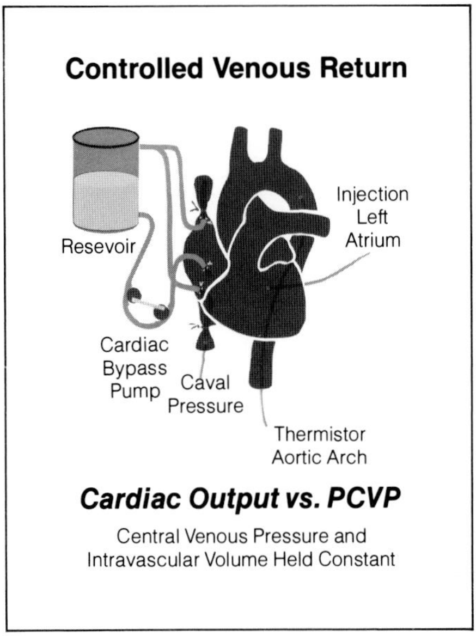

Figure 9
Surgical model for achieving controlled venous return.

Figure 10 shows the five animals studied, where cardiac index was plotted against PCVP. Although there was some difference in the slopes of the relationship from animal to animal, within each individual study the correlation was extremely tight, yielding r-values on linear regression analysis of .99, .96, .99, .97, and .99.

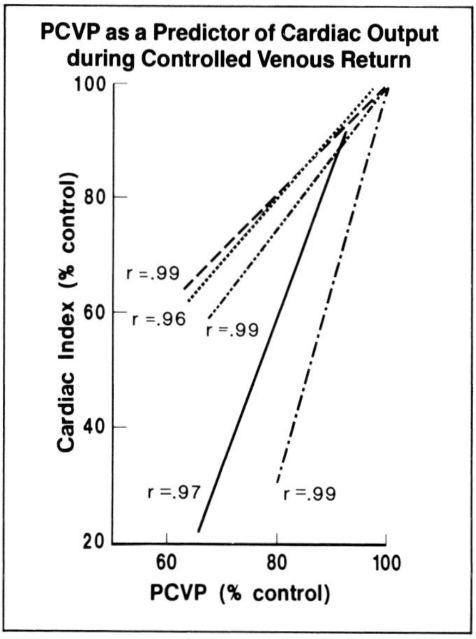

Figure 10
Correlation between PCVP and CO during controlled venous return.

This information encouraged us to look further into the utility of measuring indices of peripheral perfusion. The other parameter which we felt might be capable of meaningful information on a continuous and instantaneous basis was peripheral venous oxygen saturation, which we also measured using an Oximetrix catheter.

Since the mixed venous oxygen saturation was a very significant and sensitive indicator of hemodynamic status in our preliminary study, we evaluated the relative efficacy of venous oxygen saturation in other locations during hemorrhage. We compared the trends for central venous oxygen saturation by simply placing an Oximetrix catheter in the right atrium. There was, again, a very good correlation between $S\bar{v}O_2$ and central venous oxygen saturation. This correlation was good both in the absolute magnitude of the values we obtained and in terms of the linear relationship with the extent of hemorrhage.

Several streams of venous blood with differing oxygen saturation merge at the level of the right atrium. Although this allows for an erroneous estimation of $S\bar{v}O_2$, depending upon the sampling site, the trend of the saturation against hemodynamic disturbances will be meaningful, if the sampling site is held constant. Similarly, the peripheral venous oxygen saturation is closely related to $S\bar{v}O_2$, as shown in Figure 11.

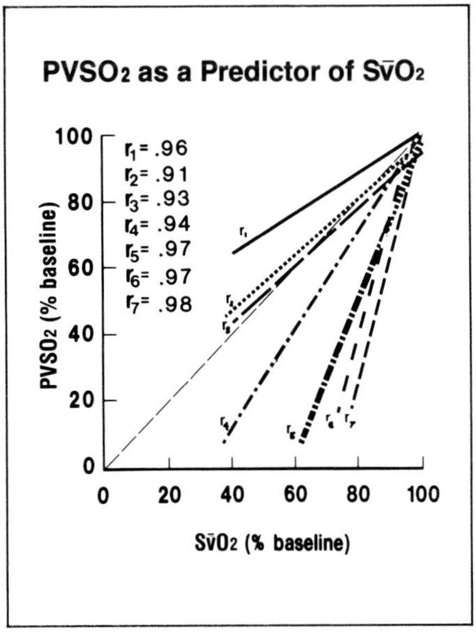

Figure 11
Correlation between $PVSO_2$ and $S\bar{v}O_2$ during hemorrhage.

There is a similar relationship between peripheral venous oxygen saturation and $S\bar{v}O_2$ to that between peripheral postcapillary venous pressure and cardiac output. Namely, that although the slopes varied from animal to animal, within each individual studied the relationship between these two parameters was extremely tight. Again, r-values ranged from .91 to .98. With the exception of the one study, the peripheral venous oxygen saturation was either equally sensitive to hemorrhage or more sensitive to hemorrhage than was the $S\bar{v}O_2$.

The efficacy of all these parameters was then studied during acute hemorrhage and resuscitation. The animals were bled to a pressure of 40 mmHg. They were held at 40 mmHg for 20 minutes and then reinfused. The hemorrhage amounted to, on the average, 50.3 ± 2.1 cc/kg. As you can see in Figure 12, during hemorrhage, PCVP fell in a very sensitive fashion. It remained low during the stabilization phase and then during the reinfusion phase rose in a near linear manner, coming exactly to baseline levels when the animal was totally repleted. In contrast, central venous pressure fell in a less sensitive fashion. It also rose linearly, but came to baseline values prematurely, on the average after only 50% of the hemorrhage volume had been reinfused such that it predicted resuscitation prematurely. In three of the ten animals studied it actually came to normal after only one-third of the hemorrhaged volume had been reinfused. Pulmonary wedge pressure similarly showed a linear relationship during the reinfusion phase. On the average, it came back to baseline after two-thirds of the hemorrhage volume had been reinfused. In two of the ten animals it came back to baseline levels after only 50% of the hemorrhage volume had been reinfused. PCVP again, on the other hand, never prematurely reflected adequate resuscitation.

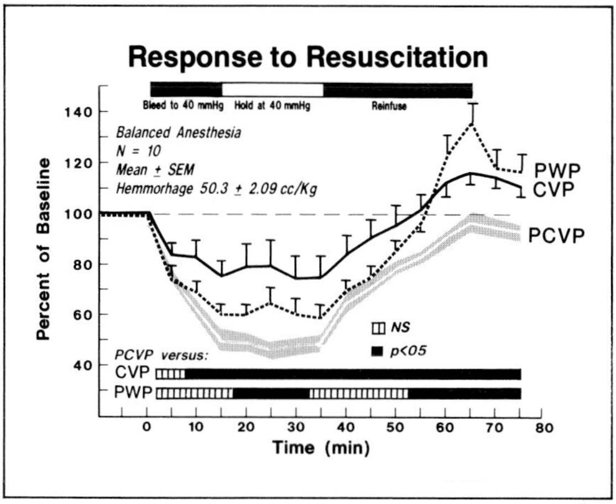

Figure 12

Relative efficacy of PCVP, PWP, and CVP in predicting the adequacy of resuscitation.

As with PCVP, $S\bar{v}O_2$ and cardiac output were excellent predictors of the adequacy of resuscitation. Figure 13 displays how cardiac output and pulmonary artery oxygen saturation fell very sensitively, rose in a linear fashion, and came back to exactly baseline levels when the animal was totally repleted.

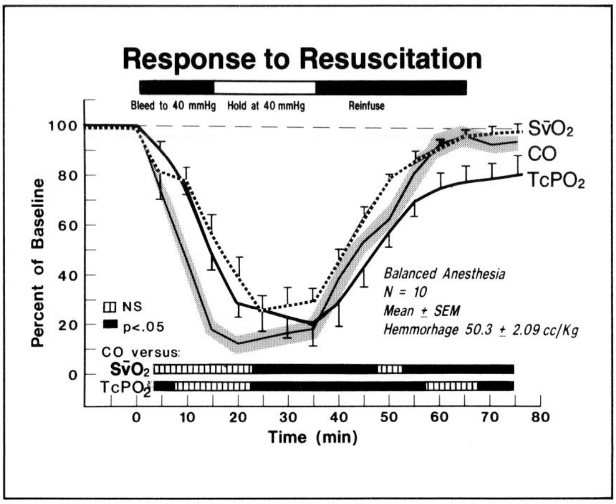

Figure 13

Relative efficacy of $S\bar{v}O_2$, CO, and $TcPO_2$ in predicting the adequacy of resuscitation.

Figure 14 compares the efficacy of the three venous oxygen saturation parameters that we have looked at: Pulmonary arterial, central venous, and peripheral venous. As you can see, the relationship is actually very similar. Meaningful information can be obtained with the catheter in the central venous system or in a peripheral venous system, at least in this model, and can accurately predict the adequacy of resuscitation. The aortic oxygen saturation, as one would expect, remained stable during the entire course of the study.

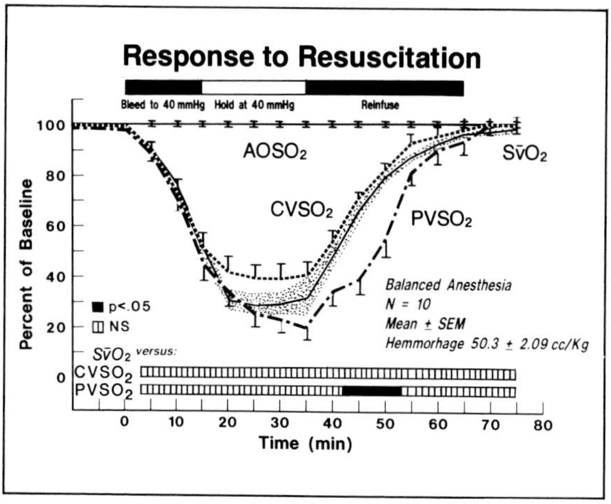

Figure 14

Relative efficacy of PVSO2, CVSO2, and S$\bar{v}$O2 in predicting the adequacy of resuscitation.

In conclusion, on the basis of this study, we feel that PCVP is probably a function of cutaneous blood flow. It appears to have a direct correlation with cardiac output. Based upon the relationship between peripheral venous oxygen saturation and S$\bar{v}$O2 we feel that peripheral venous oxygen saturation probably also has a direct correlation with cardiac output. PCVP and venous oxygen saturation were the only parameters studied which were reliably predictive of hemodynamic status without requiring a pulmonary arterial catheter. Based upon these findings we would suggest that further experimental and clinical studies are indicated.

USE OF CONTINUOUS $S\bar{v}O_2$ INTRA AND POSTOPERATIVELY IN MANAGING THE HEMODYNAMICS OF CARDIAC SURGERY PATIENTS

7

John F. Schweiss, M.D.*

We introduced our first Oximetrix fiberoptic pulmonary artery catheter in March, 1981. Since that time we have placed over 400 catheters, primarily in patients undergoing vein grafting for cardiopulmonary bypass for coronary artery disease, or in patients undergoing valve replacement. I was aware of Dr. Wayne Martin's efforts in the early 1970s, utilizing the Edwards fiberoptic catheter and the Physio-Control Oximeter, to introduce this modality some ten years ago.[1] Many of the observations he made of changes in mixed venous oxygen saturation ($S\bar{v}O_2$) related to cardiac output, oxygen consumption and oxygen availability have been observed in the patients that we have managed. I will attempt now to show you some of those changes.

The value of cardiac output, mixed venous oxygen saturation, A-V oxygen differences, stroke indices, preload and afterload determinations, and systemic and pulmonary vascular resistance are well established. These determinations, however, are done on an intermittent basis. They, unfortunately, leave gaps in our knowledge regarding the patients' status, particularly in the critically ill whose

*St. Louis University School of Medicine
Section of Anesthesiology (Surgery)
1325 South Grand Boulevard
St. Louis, Missouri 63104

circulatory dynamics are changing dramatically in the interval between observations.

Changes in $S\bar{v}O_2$, recorded on a continuous basis, will therefore trigger additional measurements to be obtained, confirming and further delineating the etiology of the changes in $S\bar{v}O_2$.

The Fick Principle, as shown in Figure 1, indicates that the mixed venous oxygen content varies directly with arterial oxygen content, oxygen uptake and cardiac output.

$$\text{Cardiac Output (L/min)} = \frac{\text{Oxygen Uptake (cc/min)}}{\text{Arterio-Venous } O_2 \text{ Difference (cc)}} \times 10$$

Example:

$$5\ \text{L/min} = \frac{250\ \text{cc/min}}{5\ \text{cc}} \times 10$$

Figure 1
The Fick Principle.

In the anesthetized state the metabolic rate, pulmonary gas exchange, and hemoglobin concentration remain fairly constant. As a consequence, during anesthesia the $S\bar{v}O_2$ will vary directly with cardic output.

In the postoperative period, however, and at times during surgery, alterations in arterial oxygen content, particularly as influenced by the hemoglobin concentration and intrapulmonary shunting, and alterations in oxygen consumption related to such factors as shivering, increased respiratory work, fever and infection may dramatically alter oxygen consumption, as well.

Figure 2a shows a 72 year old white female, a Jehovah's Witness, who refused any blood products and who underwent aortic valve replacement. She received a fentanyl, Pavulon®, oxygen anesthetic. Her prebypass $S\bar{v}O_2$ values were high. The 90% saturation is a reflection of the high oxygen tensions in her arterial blood associated with an FIO_2 of 1.0 and a reduced metabolic oxygen demand associated with paralysis and narcosis.

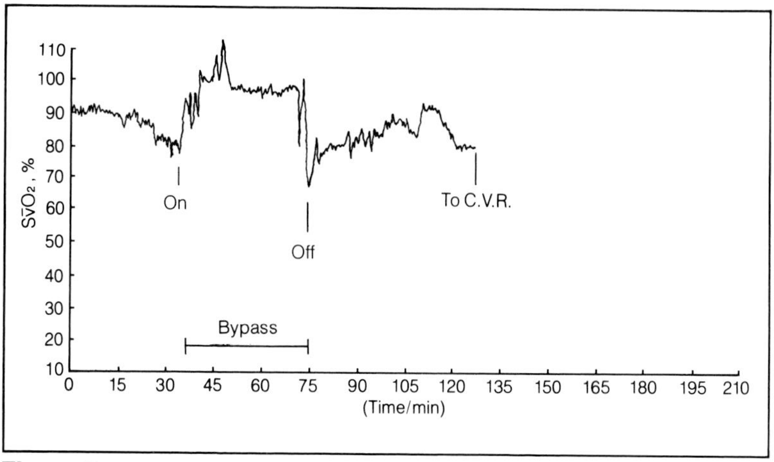

Figure 2a
H.K., 72 y.o. W.F., A.V.R., Jehovah's Witness, (B.S.A. 1.65). Pre and postbypass $S\bar{v}O_2$ within normal limits.

Figure 2b shows her postbypass $S\bar{v}O_2$ values which were initially elevated, but fell in the Cardiovascular Recovery Room (C.V.R.) despite high cardiac output and cardiac indices. Following this initial fall in the immediate postanesthetic period, they rose again to levels above 60%. We attributed this initial fall to an increased oxygen demand associated with awakening and shivering to restore normothermia.

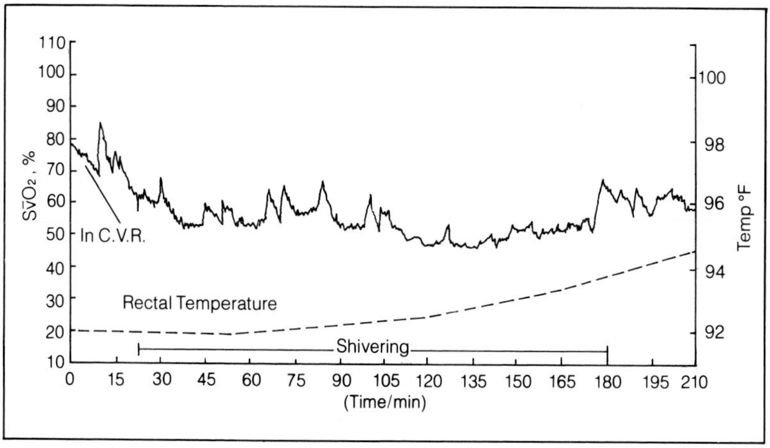

Figure 2b
H.K., 72 y.o. W.F. Decreased $S\bar{v}O_2$ due to increased metabolic demand early postoperative period (shivering).

Her hematocrit, however, continued to fall in the postoperative period, as shown in Figure 2c. A fall in $S\bar{v}O_2$ occurred with this fall in hematocrit. This was associated with a further rise in cardiac output to compensate for the reduced oxygen availability. This patient appeared asymptomatic when her $S\bar{v}O_2$ was between 40% and 45% and her hemoglobin was 6 gm%. This, then, represents a patient who was able to supply her tissue oxygen needs in spite of a diminished oxygen content of the arterial blood and low $S\bar{v}O_2$ values.

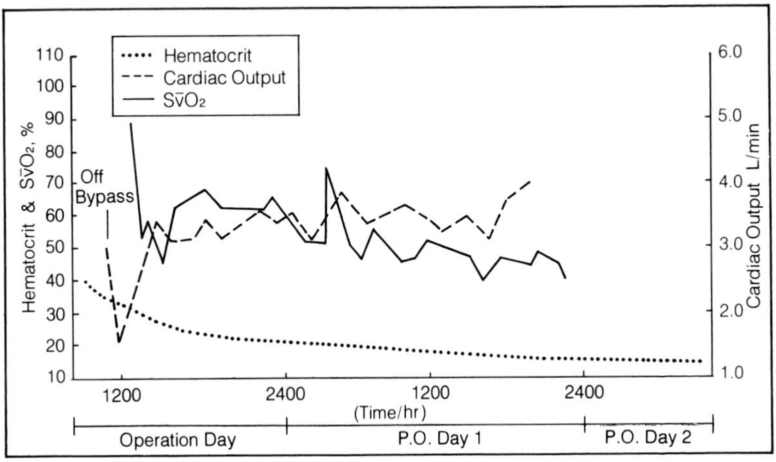

Figure 2c

H.K., 72 y.o. W.F. Decreased $S\bar{v}O_2$ due to anemia.

Figure 3a depicts a 74 year old white female, who underwent a double vein graft and left ventricular aneurysmectomy approximately four weeks after a massive infarction involving the left anterior descending artery. She was doing poorly prior to anesthesia induction. With the encouragement of her cardiologist, we undertook vein grafting and aneurysmectomy. Her immediate postbypass period necessitated the use of both inotropes and vasodilators, and the intra-aortic balloon pump (I.A.B.P.) to restore a satisfactory $S\bar{v}O_2$.

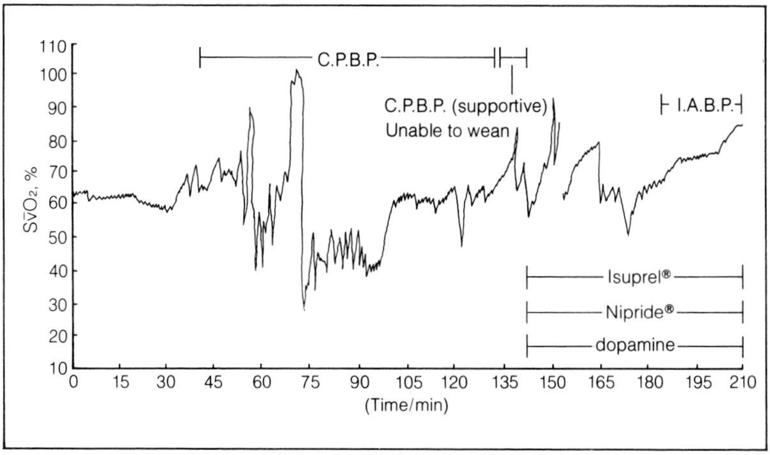

Figure 3a

G.D., 74 y.o. W.F., D.V.G. and left ventricular aneurysmectomy, post M.I. 4 weeks, (B.S.A. 1.52). Improved $S\bar{v}O_2$ with use of I.A.B.P.

Initially, her $S\bar{v}O_2$ values were reasonable, as shown in Figure 3b, but her cardiac output declined despite the continued use of inotropes, vasodilators and the I.A.B.P. Her hematocrit continued to rise, and although her $S\bar{v}O_2$ values remained above 60%, the A-V oxygen difference was 10-12 volumes %. Her cardiac output remained low, approximately 50-60% of normal, in spite of high atrial filling pressures. The use of inotropes, vasodilators and the I.A.B.P. failed to sustain this patient. Her final moments were associated with rapidly falling $S\bar{v}O_2$ from 60% to 30% and below.

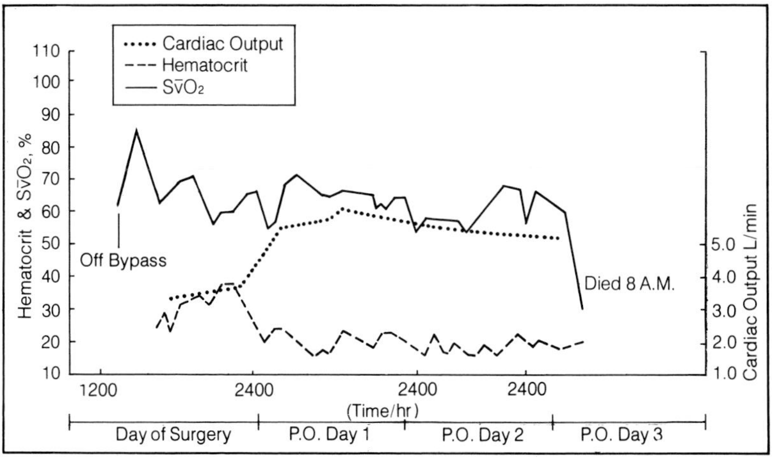

Figure 3b

G.D., 74 y.o. W.F. $S\bar{v}O_2$ 60%; rapid fall to 30% at time patient expired.

The 58 year old white male shown in Figure 4a underwent vein grafting to his right coronary and circumflex arteries. Prior to bypass he sustained a blood loss during cannulation. You can note the fall in $S\bar{v}O_2$ associated with a decrease in cardiac output. Following bypass his $S\bar{v}O_2$ values were borderline. At approximately 11:58 Nipride® was started and increased to 100 mcg/min, with some improvement. Fifty minutes later, a rapidly falling $S\bar{v}O_2$ prompted the introduction of dopamine which induced a favorable rise in his $S\bar{v}O_2$.

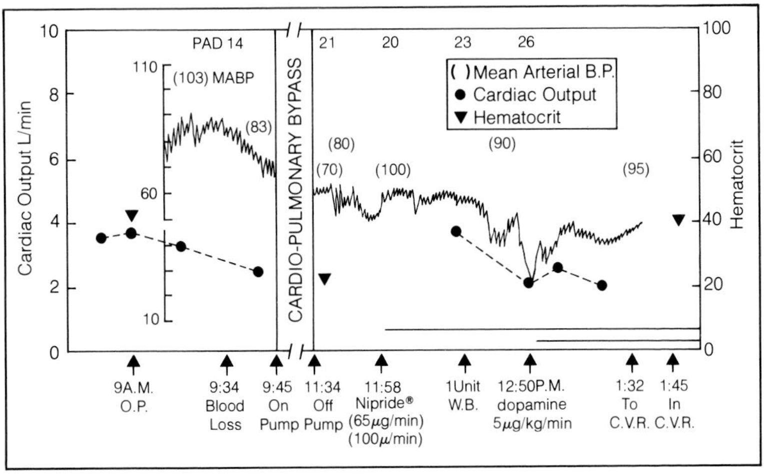

Figure 4a

Q.G., 58 y.o. WM., D.V.G. Rapidly declining $S\bar{v}O_2$ improved with dopamine, but $S\bar{v}O_2$ below 60% prior to transfer to C.V.R.

Following transfer to the C.V.R. the patient's $S\bar{v}O_2$ was noted to be low, as depicted in Figure 4b. Apresoline® was instituted, as his mean arterial blood pressure was 103 and his cardiac output was obviously decreased, indicating an increase in peripheral vascular resistance. With the administration of Apresoline®, a prompt and sustained rise in $S\bar{v}O_2$ occurred associated with a sustained rise in cardiac output. Following improvement with vasodilator therapy the patient maintained an adequate cardiac output and $S\bar{v}O_2$.

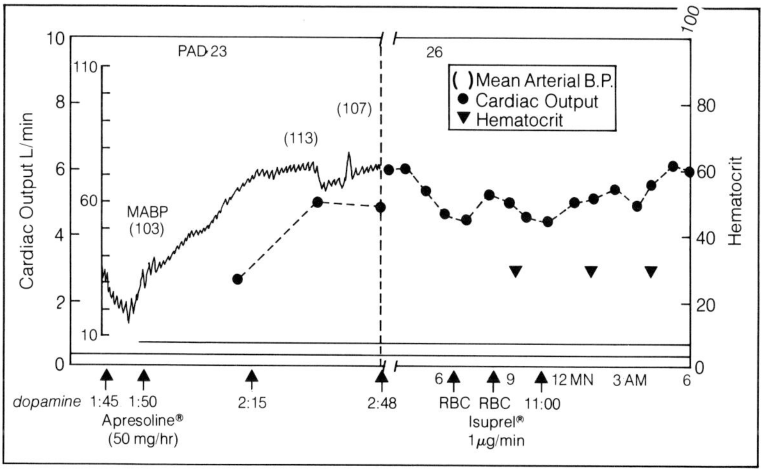

Figure 4b

Q.G., 58 y.o. W.M. Increase in $S\bar{v}O_2$ and cardiac output following Apresoline® infusion.

Figure 5 demonstrates the influence of shivering on $S\bar{v}O_2$. $S\bar{v}O_2$ fell to 45% in the latter part of the surgical intervention and was unaffected by whole blood transfusion. Following transfer to the C.V.R. there was a dramatic fall of $S\bar{v}O_2$ associated with the sitting position for taking an x-ray. Throughout the postoperative period this patient maintained an adequate cardiac index. Her $S\bar{v}O_2$ gradually returned to levels above 60%. Were we managing this patient at the present time, we would have intervened in the recovery room and administered a small dose of Pavulon® (e.g. 2-3 mgs) to determine its effect upon $S\bar{v}O_2$. The usual effect of this administration, if the fall in $S\bar{v}O_2$ is due to increased oxygen consumption associated with shivering, is a prompt return of the $S\bar{v}O_2$ to values above 60%.

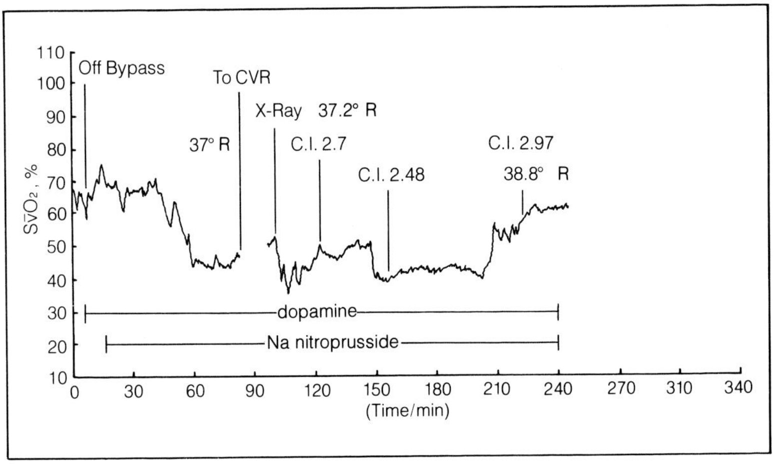

Figure 5

I.B., 57 y.o. B.F., A.V.R., (B.S.A. 2.06). Fall in $S\bar{v}O_2$ from 50% to 30% associated with sitting position during a chest x-ray. Low $S\bar{v}O_2$ attributed to shivering.

The favorable influence of 2 mg of Pavulon® on a $S\bar{v}O_2$ of 45% in the C.V.R. in a 65 year old female, who had undergone a double aorto-coronory vein graph, is depicted in Figure 6a.

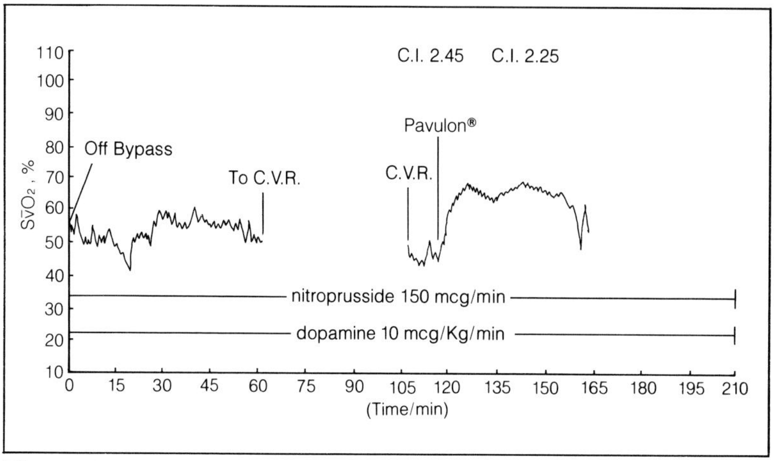

Figure 6a
M.E., 65 y.o. W.F., M.V.R. Prompt Sv̄O2 increase to 66% following Pavulon® (shivering).

Following the initial improvement this patient ultimately went downhill, as shown in Figure 6b. She expired approximately eight hours postoperatively, despite many efforts to improve her cardiac output with inotropes and vasodilator combinations, and the use of the I.A.B.P. The I.A.B.P. had to be inserted through the ascending aortic arch because of a previous aorto-bifemoral graft placement six years prior to this surgery. Her Sv̄O2 was unstable and never exceeded 60%, an ominous sign in our experience.

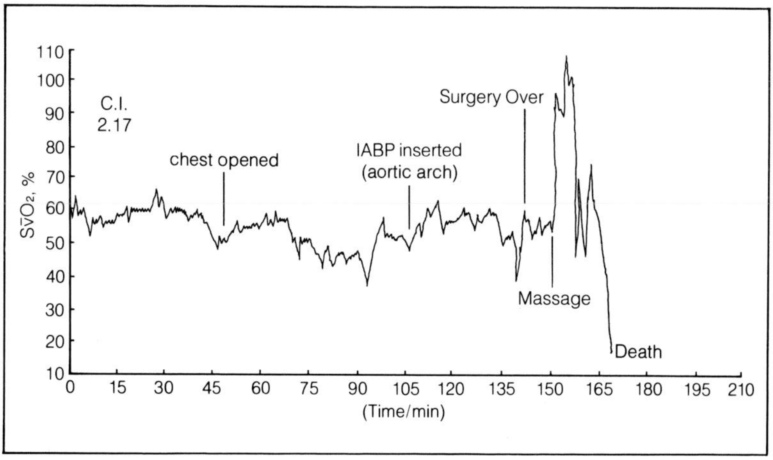

Figure 6b
M.E., 65 y.o. W.F. Terminal course in C.V.R.

The patient in Figure 7 underwent an aortic valve replacement and triple vein grafting, and was unable to be weaned from the cardiopulmonary bypass (A). Initially, we were also unable to insert an I.A.B.P. because of obstructive disease of the iliacs and femorals. Another attempt to come off bypass was unsuccessful (B). It was noted at this time, however, that her temperature was 39°, and that this temperature elevation was associated with tachycardia. A fall in $S\bar{v}O_2$ and an obvious deterioration in her cardiovascular dynamics prompted return to bypass, during which time cooling was affected to 37.5°. At this point we were able to successfully wean her from the bypass (C). With a combination of Nipride®, dopamine and Apresoline® we were able to obtain a sustained rise in $S\bar{v}O_2$ and an associated increase in cardiac output. Her course from this point was uneventful. It was our feeling that the increased oxygen demand associated with the temperature elevation and associated tachycardia, possibly attributable to the effects of dopamine, contributed to the left ventricular failure.

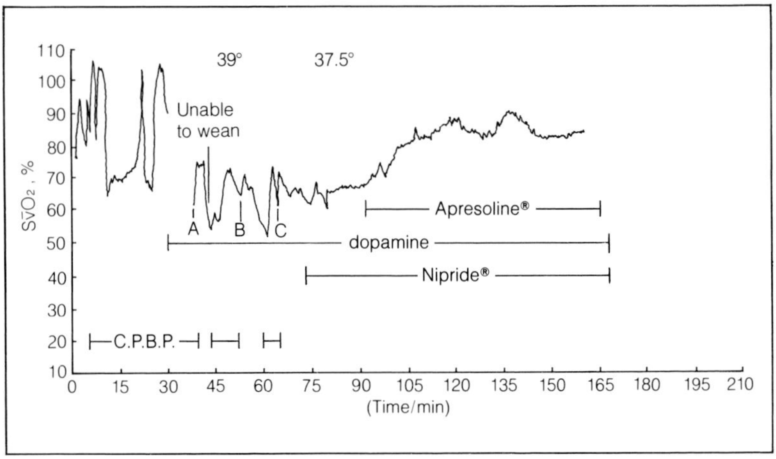

Figure 7
M.C., 61 y.o. W.F., A.V.R. and T.V.G.

The rather large male shown in Figure 8a had a fall in $S\bar{v}O_2$ in the prebypass period which responded dramatically to the administration of Nipride®. Following bypass his $S\bar{v}O_2$ slowly fell to a level of 50%. He responded dramatically to repeated 5 mg I.V. boluses of Apresoline® (total 25 mg), followed by an infusion of Apresoline® at 1 mg/10 Kg/hr. His $S\bar{v}O_2$ rose to acceptable levels of 65% or greater.

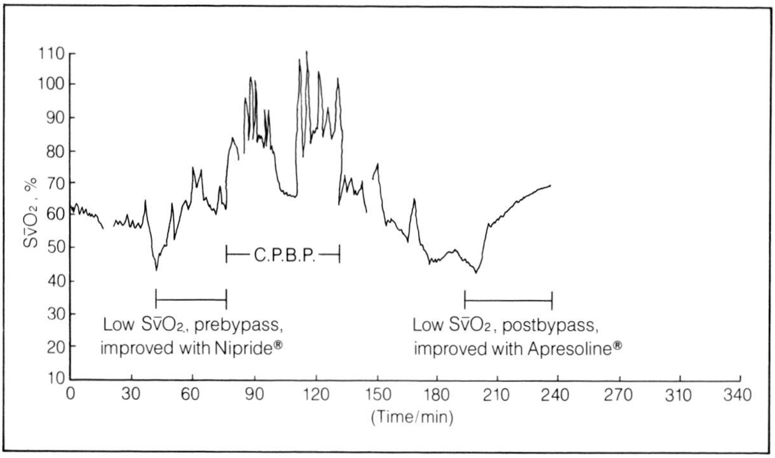

Figure 8a

D.C., T.V.G., (B.S.A. 2.09). Beneficial vasodilator response.

You can observe in Figure 8b how the cardiac output and the $S\bar{v}O_2$ followed one another in the postoperative period. The hematocrit level remained constant at 37% during this period.

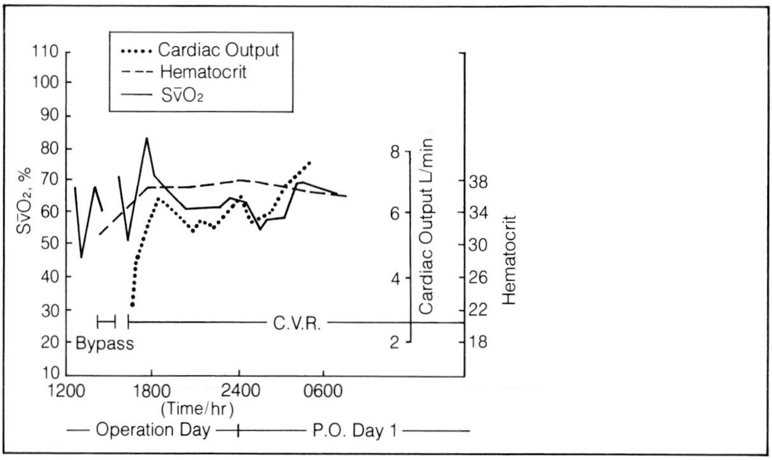

Figure 8b

D.C. $S\bar{v}O_2$ and C.O. correlation postbypass in C.V.R..

Figure 9a again shows an elderly female, postacute myocardial infarction, who underwent a left ventricular aneurysmectomy. You will note that her prebypass $S\bar{v}O_2$ values were borderline at best, at the 50%-60% range. Following bypass her $S\bar{v}O_2$ values were initially above 70%. Her saturation levels fell to 60% with sternal approximation and then gradually restored to values greater than 70% prior to transfer to the C.V.R.

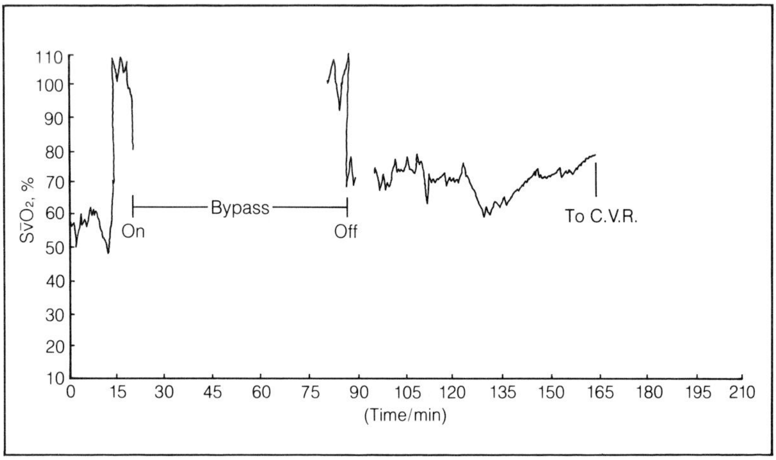

Figure 9a

M.Y., 73 y.o. B.F., left ventricular aneurysmectomy, post acute M.I., (B.S.A. 1.55).

Her tracing in the C.V.R., displayed in Figure 9b, showed the typical fall associated with a x-ray taken in the upright position. She continued to bleed postoperatively, and despite adequate amounts of transfusion and a sustained cardiac output, her $S\bar{v}O_2$ continued to fall. She was returned to the Operating Room at which time 4 mg of Pavulon® was administered, followed by a striking rise in $S\bar{v}O_2$. She was obviously shivering due to mild hypothermia from multiple transfusions. Surgical hemostasis was accomplished.

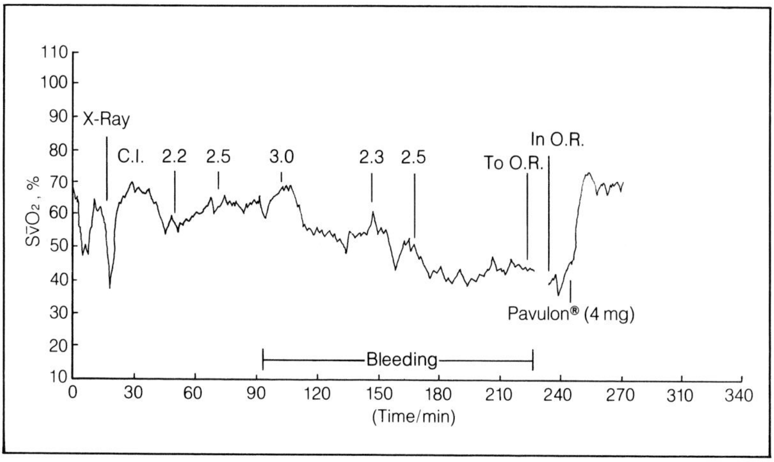

Figure 9b
M.Y., 73 y.o. B.F. Prompt return of $S\bar{v}O_2$ to normal following administration of Pavulon® in O.R..

There was a 10% fall in $S\bar{v}O_2$ associated with sternal closure, which is shown in Figure 9c.

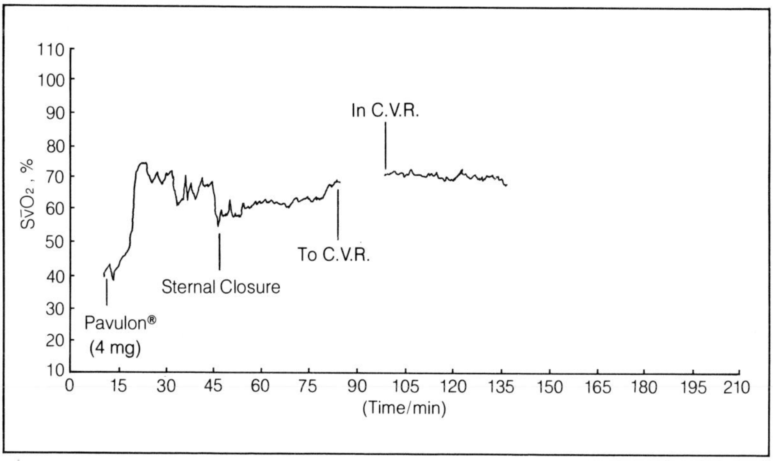

Figure 9c
M.Y., 73 y.o. B.F. $S\bar{v}O_2$ increase well maintained in O.R. and C.V.R. following surgical hemostasis.

Figure 9d graphically displays the $S\bar{v}O_2$ postoperatively. Her $S\bar{v}O_2$ remained above 65% following return to the C.V.R. Her $S\bar{v}O_2$ values remained in the normal range following extubation and mask oxygen administration, as did her cardiac index.

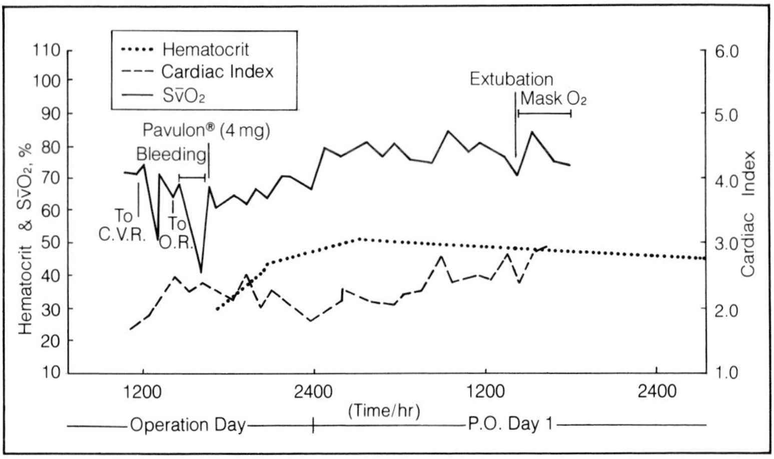

Figure 9d

M.Y., 73 y.o. B.F. $S\bar{v}O_2$, cardiac index and hematocrit values, postoperatively.

Figures 10a and 10b display the persistent downhill course of an individual who underwent ventricular aneurysmectomy in the acute phases of a myocardial infarction. Although weaning was accomplished with inotropes and mechanical support (I.A.B.P.), $S\bar{v}O_2$ remained below 60%.

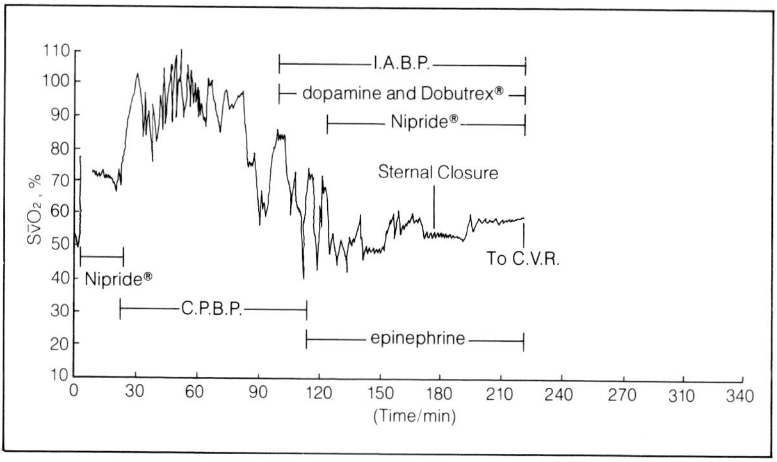

Figure 10a

M.G., 56 y.o. W.M., left ventricular aneurysmectomy for cardiogenic shock, post acute M.I. (B.S.A. 1.95).

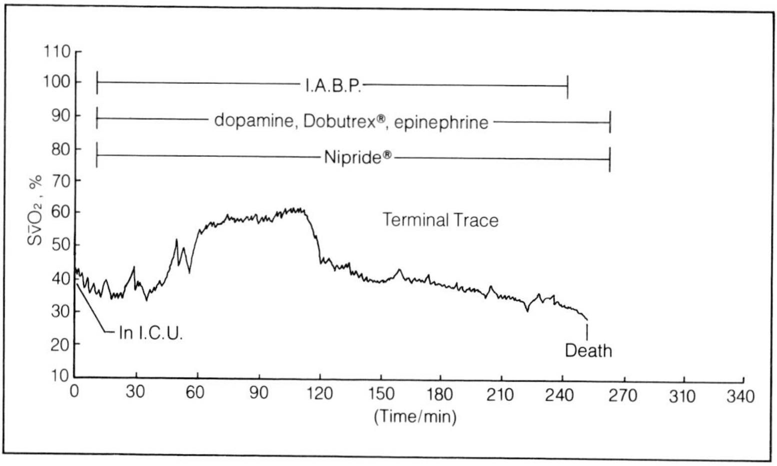

Figure 10b

M.G., 56 y.o. W.M. Downhill course to death in C.V.R..

This same patient was unable to sustain an adequate cardiac output in the postoperative period despite inotropes, vasodilators and mechanical support with an I.A.B.P., as shown in Figure 10b.

The $S\bar{v}O_2$, as displayed graphically in Figure 10c, gradually fell from 60% to 30% at the time of the terminal event.

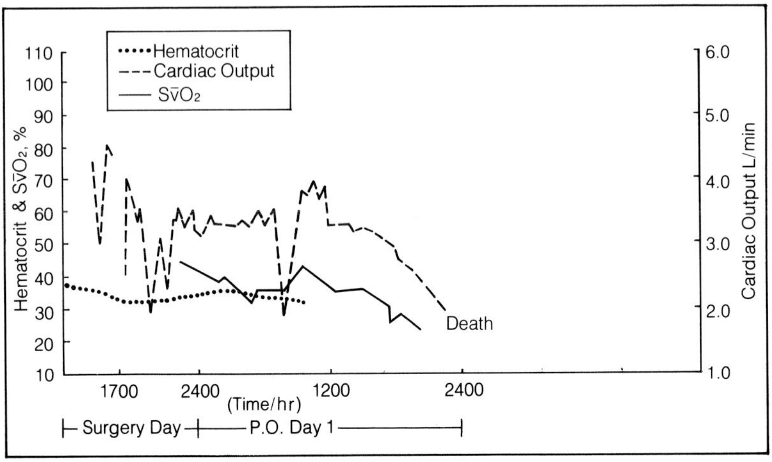

Figure 10c

M.G., 56 y.o. W.M. Cardiac output and $S\bar{v}O_2$ comparisons during postoperative downhill course to death.

You have seen representative examples of decreases in $S\bar{v}O_2$ levels that were observed with decreases in cardiac output, increases in oxygen consumption and anemia. Fortunately, arterial hypoxemia is uncommon in the bypass patient. It is also not a reliable indicator of circulatory status, but obviously if lowered could be the etiology for a decreased $S\bar{v}O_2$.

A general rule which we have followed is: If the cardiac index is greater than 2.5 L/min, all other things being appropriate (i.e. the arterial PO_2 is greater than 100 Torr and the basal metabolic rate is within normal limits), then the $S\bar{v}O_2$ should be greater than 65%, if the hematocrit is greater than 30%.

We have also observed increases in $S\bar{v}O_2$ with increases in cardiac output, with decreases in oxygen consumption (Pavulon®), as a consequence of transfusion, (at times attributable to the increased preload, but at other times as a direct consequence of an increase in oxygen content attributable to a rising hemoglobin level) and as a consequence of breathing 100% oxygen.

Figure 11 shows the effect of breathing 100% oxygen on $S\bar{v}O_2$, attributable primarily to the increase in dissolved oxygen.

EFFECT OF BREATHING 100% OXYGEN ON
MIXED VENOUS OXYGEN SATURATION*

ARTERIAL	*O_2 Tension*	*O_2 Content*	*% Sat*
Room Air	100	19.8	97.3
100% Oxygen	600	21.8	100+
VENOUS			
Room Air	36.5	13.8	70.0
100% Oxygen	42.5	15.8	78.0

*A-V Oxygen Content Difference 6 Vol %, pH 7.4, Hb 15 Gm %, 37°C.

Figure 11
Effect of breathing 100% oxygen on $S\bar{v}O_2$.

One of the common techniques employed in cardiovascular surgery is the use of 100% oxygen as the inhalant gas and a high dose narcotic technique. We were surprised at times to find that we had $S\bar{v}O_2$ values which approached 90%, and we were concerned that we had inaccuracy in the calibration of the instrument. However, a calibration check, obtained by withdrawing a sample of blood from the pulmonary artery at the time of these high levels, verified the accuracy of the determination. An increase in $S\bar{v}O_2$ to approximately 78% occurs as an effect of breathing 100% oxygen, when based on an A-V oxygen difference of 6 volumes %. When this A-V oxygen difference is reduced to 5 volumes %, the $S\bar{v}O_2$ rises to 83%. When the A-V content difference decreases to 4 volumes %, the $S\bar{v}O_2$ further rises to 88%. It would appear, then, that these high oxygen values are the result of a reduced metabolic demand in the presence of normal cardiac outputs as a consequence of the narcotic administration, a mild decrease in body temperature and an increase in dissolved oxygen.

Figure 12 illustrates the favorable effect of vasodilators and inotropes on $S\bar{v}O_2$ in the early postbypass period. The decrease in $S\bar{v}O_2$ following nitrous oxide can also be seen, even when administered in 50% concentrations. Nitrous oxide may, in addition to reducing the inspired oxygen content and the quantity of oxygen dissolved in the plasma, have a negative inotropic effect, particularly in these unstable cardiovascular patients. Its administration may at times precipitate profound falls in blood pressure and reduce cardiac output. $S\bar{v}O_2$ falls below normal levels when this occurs. The fall in $S\bar{v}O_2$ is probably an indication for the discontinuance of nitrous oxide.

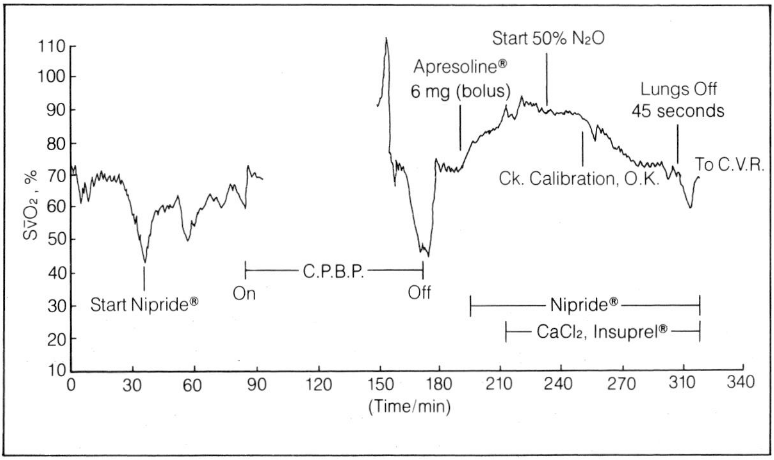

Figure 12

E.F., 38 y.o. W.M., M.V.R. Favorable effect of vasodilator and inotrope therapy; $S\bar{v}O_2$ fall with N_2O.

Figure 13 depicts a patient who responded dramatically to the use of the I.A.B.P. following an acute episode of left ventricular failure. Mechanical support in this instance was associated with restoration of a satisfactory $S\bar{v}O_2$, which was sustained in the postoperative period. The increase in $S\bar{v}O_2$ following the initiation of Isuprel® is clearly evident as a beneficial maneuver.

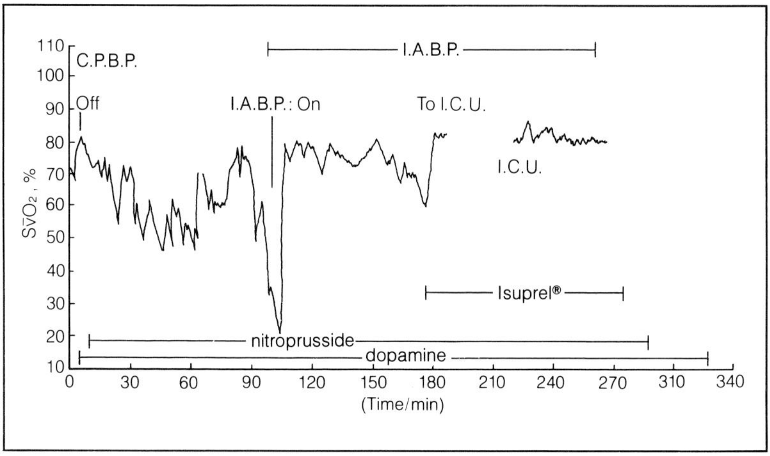

Figure 13
E.R., 55 y.o. W.F., acute left ventricular failure, postbypass, (B.S.A. 1.5).

We have observed transient changes in $S\bar{v}O_2$ values as a consequence of many common maneuvers that occur in the postoperative period. These falls average about 15% and are listed below in Figure 14.

MIXED VENOUS OXYGEN SATURATION
OXIMETRIX
TRANSIENT CHANGES

Observations	% Decreases
Suctioning	−14.7 ±7.1
Voluntary movement	−15.5 ±6.4
Coughing	−15.1 ±3.3
X-ray (sitting up)	− 9.1 ±4.6
Extubation	−15.3 ±5.7
C.P.A.P.	− 5.0 ±1.4
Bleeding	−24.0 ±2.8
Shivering	−22.7 ±4.2
Chest physiotherapy	−20.5 ±3.5
Sternal closure	−16.0 ±5.7
Vomiting	−18.0 ±2.0
Heart block	−30.0

Figure 14
Transient changes in $S\bar{v}O_2$ values.

Restoration to the pre-event level usually occurs in five to seven minutes. Some events such as bleeding, shivering, and heart block will persist until corrected. It is somewhat reassuring at the time of weaning and extubation to be able to correlate the various maneuvers with the $S\bar{v}O_2$.

Figure 15 illustrates an individual, post aorto-coronary vein grafting, with an 18% saturation decline associated with suctioning, a return to a level 7% above presuctioning values, and a 6% fall associated with the discontinuing of mechanical ventilation and the institution of C.P.A.P. A transient fall occurred during extubation, followed by a sustained rise to the levels present during C.P.A.P.

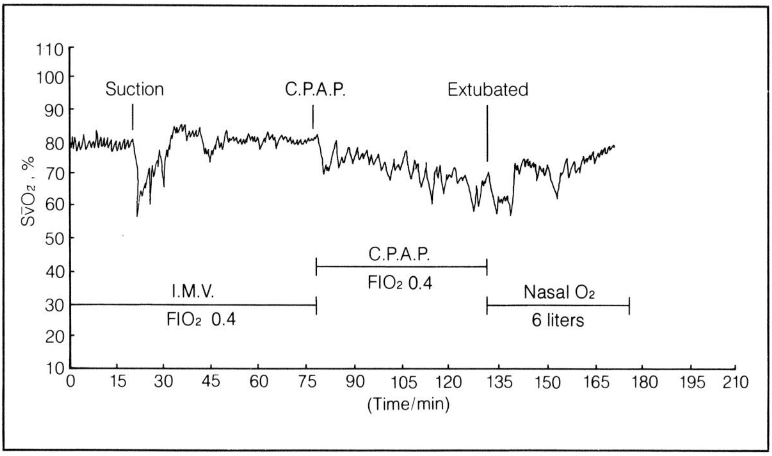

Figure 15

D.B., 62 y.o. W.M., postvein graft. Effects of suctioning, C.P.A.P., extubation and nasal O_2.

The effects of repeated endotracheal suctioning on a patient in the C.V.R. who had undergone mitral valve replacement for end-stage mitral disease are seen in Figure 16. Suctioning was not repeated until the $S\bar{v}O_2$ had returned to the presuction value, which in this instance took five to seven minutes. Following the suctioning her $S\bar{v}O_2$ values remained higher by 6%, an indication of some persistent improvement in oxygen delivery.

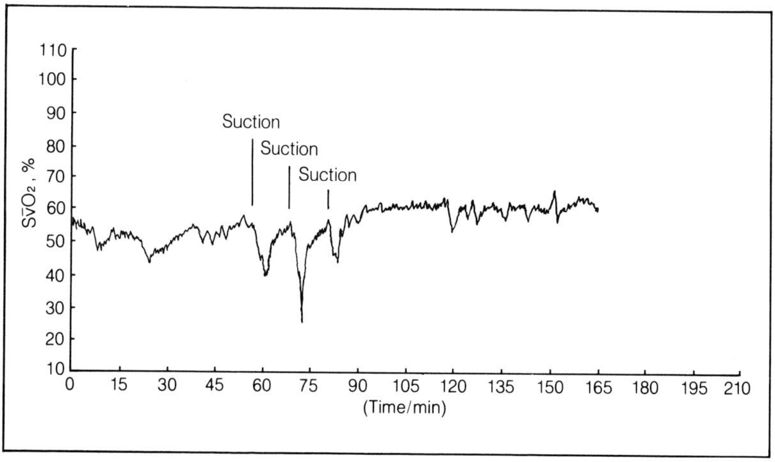

Figure 16
M.S., M.V.R. Improvement in S$\bar{v}O_2$ following repeated endotracheal suctioning.

Figure 17 depicts a patient who had an episode of acute bleeding shortly after bypass. Her S$\bar{v}O_2$ fell acutely to critical levels, but it was restored promptly by hemostasis, the administration of packed cells and replacement of the lost blood by scavenging and reinfusion. Following this hypotensive episode, her S$\bar{v}O_2$ level was well maintained. We were unable to do a cardiac output due to a thermodilution thermistor failure, which was exchanged at the conclusion of surgery.

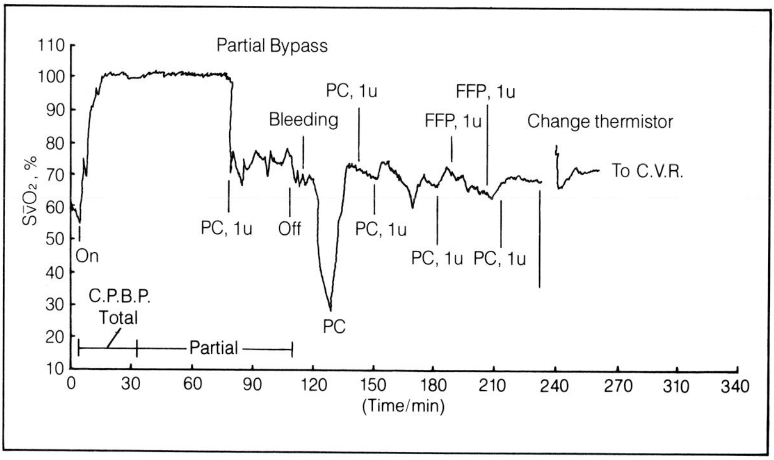

Figure 17
M.B., 63 y.o. W.F., M.V.R. S$\bar{v}O_2$ fall with acute blood loss; restoration with blood volume replacement.

Figure 18 illustrates an individual who also sustained a blood loss which was associated with a fall in $S\bar{v}O_2$. The patient responded to transfusion, but the $S\bar{v}O_2$ levels remained in the vicinity of 50%. We ultimately instituted vasodilator therapy with Apresoline®. The prompt rise in $S\bar{v}O_2$ occurred as a consequence of repeated bolus administration of Apresoline®. The sustained rise persisted following admission into the C.V.R.

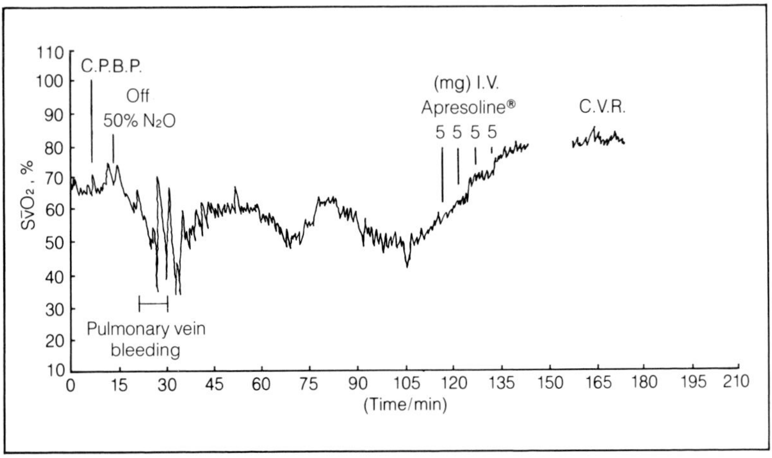

Figure 18

A.C., 59 y.o. W.M., 4 V.G. Sustained $S\bar{v}O_2$ rise with Apresoline® prior to transfer to C.V.R.

The patient illustrated in Figure 19 had undergone an aortic valve replacement and triple vein graft. She showed evidence of a declining $S\bar{v}O_2$ in the early postoperative period. She manifested signs of left ventricular failure and required a left ventricular filling pressure of 26-28 mmHg to maintain an adequate cardiac output and vascular dynamics in the Operating Room. We failed to maintain her filling pressure at this level in the C.V.R. When her left atrial pressure fell to 20, her $S\bar{v}O_2$ had fallen to 45%. She fibrillated at this point, but responded favorably to epinephrine, external massage and defibrillation. We, fortuitously, had called for more blood when her $S\bar{v}O_2$ and left atrial filling pressure were declining. It arrived just prior to the onset of ventricular fibrillation. With additional volume replacement, her $S\bar{v}O_2$ remained above the critical level, thereafter.

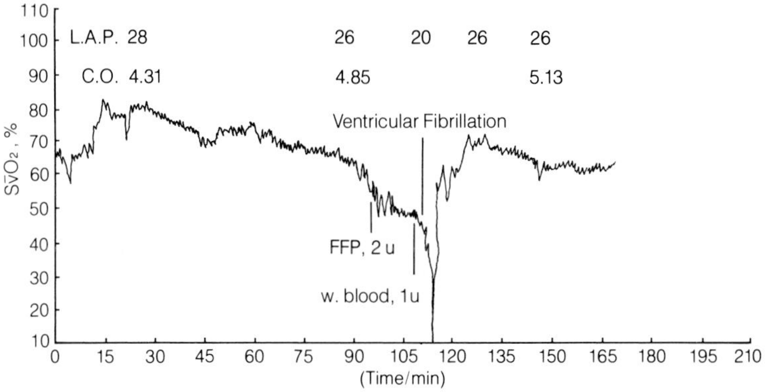

Figure 19

M.V., 73 y.o. W.F., A.V.R. and T.V.G., (B.S.A. 16). Ventricular fibrillation following fall in L.A.P. from 26 Torr to 20 Torr.

The patient illustrated in Figure 20 presented an interesting experience for us. Approximately seven or eight minutes after passage of the catheter into her pulmonary artery, her $S\bar{v}O_2$ was approximately 70%. At that point her saturation rose to above 100%. Initially, I thought we had floated into a wedge position, and I pulled the catheter back 2 cm. In viewing the monitor at that time, it was apparent that not only had her $S\bar{v}O_2$ fallen to 80%, but that there was also no pulmonary artery trace and no electrical activity other than that of ventricular fibrillation. Massage was instituted and only then did the $S\bar{v}O_2$ fall to the 10 to 20% levels observed here. Following defibrillation and restoration of circulation you can observe the prompt return of the $S\bar{v}O_2$ to the prearrest levels. She was prepped, the chest was opened and bypass instituted. Following bypass, despite the use of dopamine and Isuprel®, she was unable to be weaned from bypass on the initial attempt. A bolus dose of 50 mcg of epinephrine and 100 mg of Xylocaine® improved cardiac contractility dramatically. She was readily weaned on the next attempt. She sustained her $S\bar{v}O_2$ above 80% thereafter, with small amounts of dopamine (5 mcg/Kg/min) and Isuprel® (1.5 mcg/min).

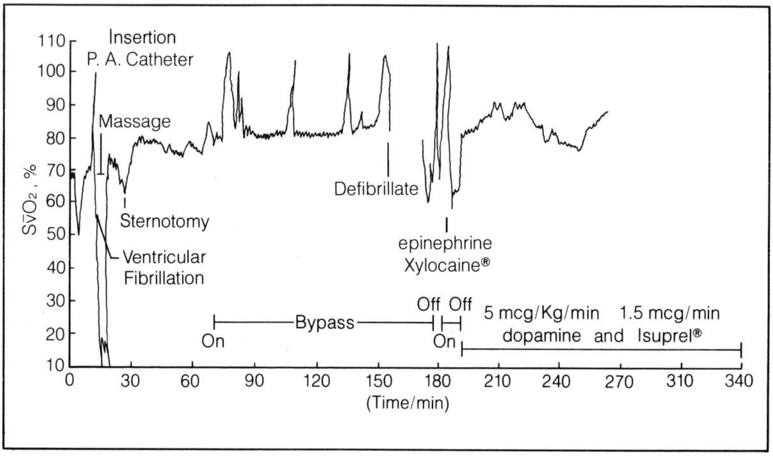

Figure 20

P.F., 36 y.o. W.F., M.V.R., (B.S.A. 1.6). $S\bar{v}O_2$ changes during acute ventricular fibrillation and weaning.

Figure 21 represents a misadventure. Bypass was discontinued at approximately 6:05 P.M. There was gradual decline in the S$\bar{v}O_2$ to 70%. His abdomen showed the roundness of increased abdominal tone. A modest dose of Pavulon® was administered, with a prompt rise of 12% to a S$\bar{v}O_2$ of 82%. At approximately 7:04 P.M. a bolus dose of Apresoline® was administered. His blood pressure at this time was 170/90. Unfortunately, when I removed the ampule from the drawer in which Apresoline® is kept, an ampule of epinephrine had been mixed with the other ampules of Apresoline®. A quarter cc of 1:1,000 or 250 mcg of epinephrine was inadvertently administered intravenously. The consequences of that maneuver are clearly evident. There was an immediate rise of systolic blood pressure from 130 to 220. The pulmonary artery pressure rose from 35/15 to 80/50, and there was a dramatic fall in the S$\bar{v}O_2$ from 82% to 52%. The Nipride® infusion was increased from 50 mcg/min to 150 mcg/min. The S$\bar{v}O_2$ returned to the premisadventure level and was sustained following transfer to the recovery area. We were fortunate that this individual did not fibrillate.

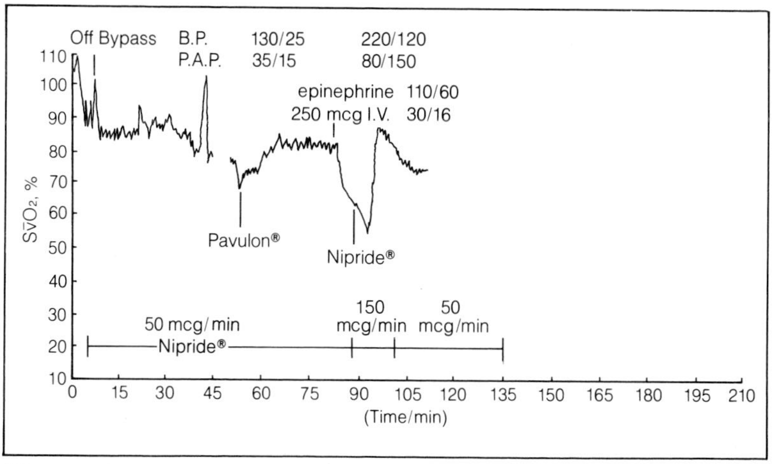

Figure 21

J.C., 54 y.o. W.M., T.V.G. S$\bar{v}O_2$ changes associated with an intravenous bolus of 250 mcg epinephrine.

We have observed sustained falls in S$\bar{v}O_2$ with postoperative bleeding, cardiac tamponade, decreases in cardiac output, hypotension, cardiac arrhythmias, shivering, and expect a fall in S$\bar{v}O_2$ should arterial hypoxemia develop.

Normally, the $S\bar{v}O_2$ should be 60% or above. If the $S\bar{v}O_2$ is falling, or if it has fallen to a level less than 50%, we immediately institute appropriate therapy and check the cardiac output, the arterial PO_2, the left atrial pressure or pulmonary capillary wedge pressure, and the peripheral vascular resistance to identify the etiology of the change. We might also draw a mixed venous oxygen sample for analysis to verify the accuracy of our instrumentation.

It is apparent that cardiac output provides the clue to adequacy of circulation, but the intermittent information is inadequate for following the critically ill. $S\bar{v}O_2$ is a continuous modality with moment to moment feedback on tissue oxygen uptake, delivery and availability.

An unsatisfactory postoperative course in patients following cardiopulmonary bypass is frequently associated with evidence of reduced cardiac output. This reduced cardiac output can be delineated by measurement of cardiac output, the A-V oxygen difference, venous oxygen saturation, arterial saturation, or hemodynamic alterations, but is most readily followed by the continuous recording oximeter from a pulmonary artery catheter.

Although we have encountered some technical problems, wedging and wall artifact are readily identified by the intensity monitoring system. Fiber damage has occurred only rarely. We have not been bothered by clot formation on the catheter. Thermistor failure has occurred on only one or two occasions. We were unable to enter the pulmonary artery from the right ventricle occasionally in our early experience, but the more flexible catheter, available since January, 1982 from Oximetrix, has not posed these problems. Drift is rare, and *in vivo* recalibration can readily be accomplished.

You will note that the 60% level is, fortuitously, in the center of the recording paper. We have a rule in our C.V.R.: If the trace is above the center of the paper (i.e. greater than 60%), the patient is probably not at great risk, unless it was higher and falling. If, however, the tracing is between 50% and 60%, it is obviously bothersome and the cause should be elucidated and treated. Should the trace fall to the 40-50% level, some therapeutic maneuvers must be initiated or the level will fall below 40%. At this point the patient is in danger of dying, unless the fall is associated with shivering. Should the trace show evidence of a rapid decline, catastrophe is imminent and immediate intervention is required. Acute cardiac death is rare when $S\bar{v}O_2$ is above 60%, unless an arrhythmia occurs but increases dramatically as the $S\bar{v}O_2$ approaches 30%.

We are extremely pleased with this modality for following patients intraoperatively and postoperatively. We feel that it has contributed significantly to patient safety. It has allowed us to intervene earlier and provide corrective measures due to an earlier appreciation of adverse changes. We currently have six units. We use them in individuals who are undergoing valve replacement, in those patients who show evidence of ventricular impairment preoperatively, or in individuals with known high-risk factors such as left main coronary artery disease or a history of left ventricular failure. Our indications for using the Opticath® pulmonary artery catheter are broadening, and the C.V.R. nurses would like them in all patients who have conventional, thermodilution pulmonary artery catheters in place.

The table shown in Figure 22, taken from Parr and Kirklin's work in 1975, demonstrated the correlation between mixed venous oxygen tensions and acute deaths.[2] You will note that above a venous tension of 35 mmHg there were no deaths. Between 30 mm and 35 mm there was one death in 34 patients of an acute nature, an incidence of 3%. Below 30 mm the incidence rose dramatically, and was 100% at values under 20 mmHg.

Table 4

Mortality vs. Mixed Venous PO_2

	Total cases	Total deaths		Acute cardiac death	
	no.	No.	Percent	No.	Percent
$P\bar{v}O_2 < 20$	2	2	100	2	100
$20 \leqq P\bar{v}O_2 < 25$	6	1	17	1	17
$25 \leqq P\bar{v}O_2 < 30$	13	2*	15.4	1	7.7
$30 \leqq P\bar{v}O_2 < 35$	34	6†	17.6	1	3
$35 \leqq P\bar{v}O_2$	25	3‡	12	0	0
Total	80	14	17.5	5	6.2

*1 patient died of hemorrhagic pulmonary edema

†1 patient died of hemorrhagic pulmonary edema
3 patients died of hypoxemia
1 patient died of gram negative sepsis

‡2 patients died of hemorrhagic pulmonary edema
1 patient died of transfusion reaction

Figure 22*

Correlation of mixed venous oxygen tension with acute death.

*Reprinted with permission from the American Heart Association, Inc. Parr G.V.S., Blackstone E.H., Kirklin J.W.: Cardiac performance and mortality after intracardiac surgery in infants and children. Circulation 51:867, 1975.

If one attempts to correlate oxygen saturations with these tensions, as displayed in Figure 23, you will note that 60% saturation represents a PO_2 of approximately 32 mmHg, and a value of 50% saturation represents a value of 26.5 mmHg.

OXYGEN TENSION VS HbO_2 SATURATION

% Sat	PO_2 Torr
80	44.5
70	36.5
60	32
50	26.5
40	23
30	19

*At pH 7.4, 37°C.

Figure 23
Correlation of oxygen saturation and oxygen tension values.

We have for this reason arbitrarily chosen the value of 60% saturation as the lower limit of normal. Any values below this level require assessment, as shown in Figure 24.

OXYGEN TENSION VS HbO_2 SATURATION

PO_2	HbO_2	Approx %
100	97.3	95 or more
90	96.4	
80	96.0	
70	93	93
60	90	90
50	85	85
40	75	75
30	58	60
25	45	45
20	31	30

*At pH 7.4

Figure 24
Lower limit of normal $S\bar{v}O_2$.

The Parr and Kirklin paper, from which a table is shown in Figure 25, also correlated cardiac index with acute cardiac death.[2] It confirmed the value of a cardiac index of greater than 2.0 liters as being associated with a high probability of survival; and it confirmed an index lower than 2.0 liters, particularly below 1.5 liters, as being associated with a high probability of an acute cardiac death.

Mortality Early After Cardiac Surgery

Table 2

Mortality vs. Measured Cardiac Index

	Total cases	Total mortality		Acute cardiac death	
	no.	No.	Percent	No.	Percent
$CI < 1.0$	6	6	100	6	100
$1.0 \leqq CI < 1.5$	10	4	40	4	40
$1.5 \leqq CI < 2.0$	18	4*	22	3	16.7
$2.0 \leqq CI < 2.5$	42	4†	10	2	4.8
$2.5 \leqq CI < 3.0$	30	4‡	13	0	0
$3.0 \leqq CI$	33	5§	15	1	3
Total	139	27	19.4	16	11.5

*Patient died of massive hepatic necrosis (preventable)

†Patient died of gram negative sepsis (preventable); Patient died of hemorrhagic pulmonary edema

‡Patients died of hypoxemia (preventable); Patient died of hemorrhagic pulmonary edema

§Patients died of hemorrhagic pulmonary edema; Patient died of transfusion reaction (preventable)

Figure 25*

Correlation of cardiac index with acute cardiac death.

*Reprinted with permission from the American Heart Association, Inc. Parr G.V.S., Blackstone E.H., Kirklin J.W.: Cardiac performance and mortality after intracardiac surgery in infants and children. Circulation 51:867, 1975.

Figure 26, from work reported by Drs. Waller and Kaplan (1982) utilizing the Oximetrix fiberoptic pulmonary artery catheter, shows a highly significant relationship between changes in $S\bar{v}O_2$ and alterations in cardiac index.[3] A 5% change in $S\bar{v}O_2$ correlated with a .5 L/min/M^2 change in cardiac index. A 15% rise in $S\bar{v}O_2$ was associated with an approximate 2 L/min/M^2 increase in cardiac index; a 10% fall in $S\bar{v}O_2$ was associated with a 1.2 L/min/M^2 decline in cardiac index. There was considerable scatter in their values. I am not completely convinced that a 10% fall in $S\bar{v}O_2$ is associated with greater than 1.2 L/min/M^2 fall in cardiac index in all patients.

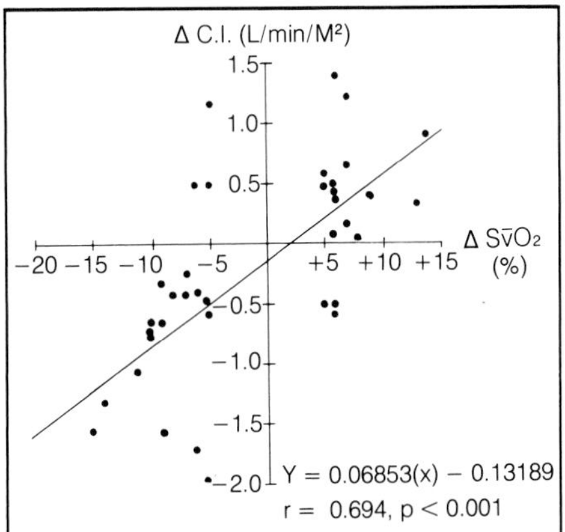

Correlation of on-line $S\bar{v}O_2$ changes measured by Opticath with corresponding changes in cardiac index. There were 39 instances during study when $S\bar{v}O_2$ values changed by 5% or more, declining 21 times and increasing 18 times. Cardiac index did not change in same direction in only seven instances.

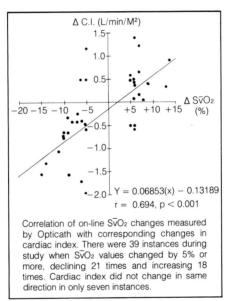

Figure 26*
Relationship between changes in $S\bar{v}O_2$ *and alterations in cardiac index.*

In summary, the recording of continuous $S\bar{v}O_2$ allows the immediate benefits of drug therapy (inotropes and vasodilators), blood volume expansion, pacemakers, mechanical augmentation and other maneuvers to be readily followed, confirming their efficacy and appropriateness.

*Reprinted with permission from Anesthesia and Analgesia. Waller J.L., Kaplan J.A., Bauman D.I., Carver J.M.: Clinical evaluation of a new fiberoptic catheter oximeter during cardiac surgery. Anest. Analg. 61:676-9, 1982.

REFERENCES

1. Martin W.E., Cheung P.W., Johnson C.C., Wong K.C.: Continuous monitoring of mixed venous oxygen saturation in man. Anesth. Analg., Current Researches 52:5, 784-793, 1973.
2. Parr G.V.S., Blackstone E.H., Kirklin J.W.: Cardiac performance and mortality early after intracardiac surgery in infants and children. Circulation 51: 867, 1975.
3. Waller J.L., Kaplan J.A., Bauman D.I., Carver J.M.: Clinical evaluation of a new fiberoptic catheter oximeter during cardiac surgery. Anesth. Analg. 61:676-9, 1982.

AN OVERALL CLINICAL ASSESSMENT OF THE ROLE OF CONTINUOUS $S\bar{v}O_2$ MEASUREMENT IN HEMODYNAMIC MONITORING IN THE ICU

8

Patrick Fahey, M.D.*

The objective of this presentation is to relate our experience using the Oximetrix pulmonary artery catheter (Opticath® optical, flow-directed pulmonary artery catheter) at Loyola University Medical Center in Chicago. Our data is based on 68 consecutive catheters used during the period November 1981 through April 1982. I emphasize that the catheters were utilized purely in a clinical setting for monitoring critically ill patients in the Intensive Care Unit. They were not part of an organized research protocol. We did not devote inordinate time checking their function, and we had no vested interest in the performance of the product. We approached the catheter as interested clinicians eager to have a reliable instrument for continuous measurement of mixed venous oxygen saturation ($S\bar{v}O_2$). Our use of the catheter was a real life experience in a busy clinical setting quite comparable to what many of you are involved in presently. We were particularly interested in the performance of the catheter in the following categories: 1) Ease of Insertion, 2) Function and Reliability, 3) Accuracy, 4) Clinical Usefulness, and 5) Cost-Effectiveness.

*Loyola University Medical Center
Pulmonary Division
2160 S. First Avenue
Maywood, Illinois 60153

INSERTION

Insertion of the Oximetrix pulmonary artery catheter was carried out in a variety of settings: Medical Intensive Care, Coronary Care, Burn Unit and the Cardiac Catheterization Laboratory. Invidividuals responsible for insertion ranged from senior staff people to fellows, early in their training. Despite the wide variety of settings and experience of the personnel, catheter placement was accomplished in all 68 attempts. The average time from insertion to pulmonary artery recording was less than ten minutes. In no instance was fluoroscopy required.

FUNCTION AND RELIABILITY

The fiberoptic bundle of two catheters crimped and broke where the catheter inserts into the optic module. This prevented display of the $S\bar{v}O_2$. These disruptions occurred early in our experience with the catheter. As we became more vigilant in assuring adequate support of the optic module, there were no further complications. The other 66 catheters functioned normally until clinical conditions permitted their removal. Balloon rupture did not occur in any of the 68 catheters. The mean duration of usage for 23 catheters used in the Medical Intensive Care Unit was 6.1 days. Two catheters were in place longer than ten days and operated normally.

A safety feature of the catheter is its ability to detect impingement on the blood vessel wall. When the optical signal deflects off blood vessel endothelium instead of red blood cells, the intensity signal flashes and a recording of low intensity is made. The $S\bar{v}O_2$ reading frequently is noted to be falsely high. We believe that this early warning of catheter impingement on the vessel lumen may prevent or lessen the occurrence of pulmonary infarction associated with pulmonary artery catheters. I suspect we greatly underestimate the occurrence of pulmonary artery catheter-associated infarction and thrombosis. By prompt respositioning of the catheter this complication should be avoided.

ACCURACY

We assessed the accuracy of the Oximetrix pulmonary artery catheter by daily comparison of its recorded value with a 5 cc sample of venous blood aspirated simultaneously through the distal tip of the catheter and immediately measured on a IL 280 Co-Oximeter. Comparison of 62 samples, as displayed in Figure 1, showed a high degree of correlation over a range of saturation from 35% to 80% (r=0.92).

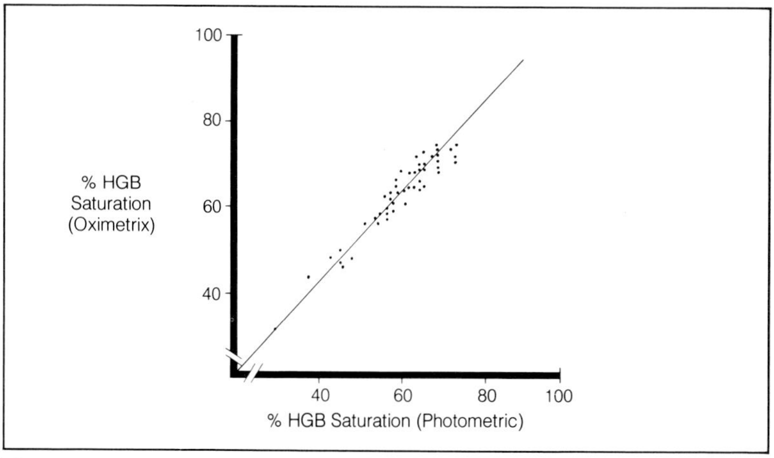

Figure 1

CLINICAL USEFULNESS

We found the Oximetrix pulmonary artery catheter extremely useful in a variety of clinical settings for providing accurate and reliable measurements of $S\bar{v}O_2$.

Ventilator Management Figure 2 displays the recording of a 56 year old male recovering from bilateral lower lobe pneumococcal pneumonia. He removed his face mask supply of 0.40 FIO_2 to eat lunch. Note the prompt decrease in $S\bar{v}O_2$ from 68% to 55%. The time from the removal of the face mask to the onset of decline of $S\bar{v}O_2$ was less than one minute. The catheter has a fast response time.

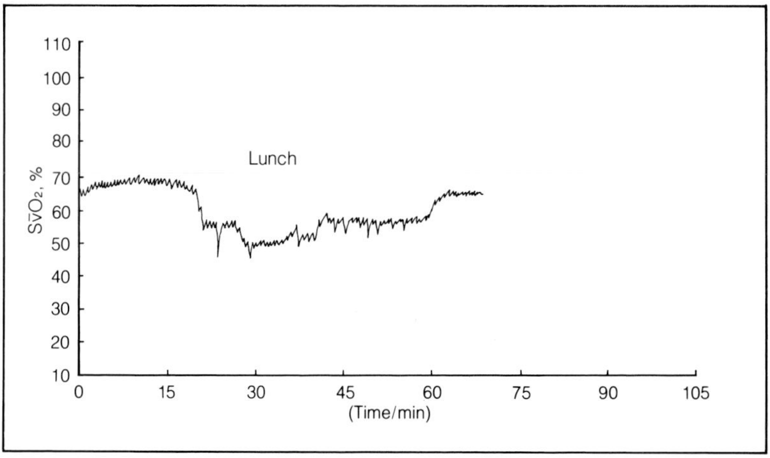

Figure 2

Figure 3 is the record of a 60 year old female with adult respiratory syndrome due to aspiration pneumonia. She was receiving FIO_2 of 0.80. The initial $S\bar{v}O_2$ was 48%. With the addition of 5 cms of PEEP it increased to 55%, and with 10 cms to 65%. Corresponding arterial PO_2 values were 41 mmHg, 50 mmHg and 82 mmHg. Since $S\bar{v}O_2$ was a key indicator of the adequacy of tissue oxygenation, we titrated changes in FIO_2 and PEEP by noting their affect on $S\bar{v}O_2$.

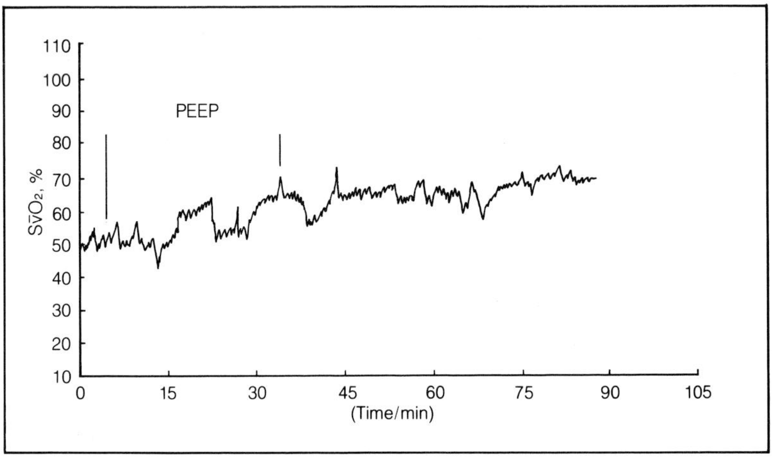

Figure 3

Trends in Cardiac Output With patients in the Coronary Care Unit, abrupt changes in $S\bar{v}O_2$ often heralded changes in cardiac output. These patients frequently had relatively normal lungs and normal arterial blood gases. Figure 4 shows a 45 year old male who had a $S\bar{v}O_2$ of 63%, but following complaints of chest pain this patient exhibited a marked decrease in $S\bar{v}O_2$ to 50%. This was accompanied by a decrease in blood pressure from 90 mmHg to 50 mmHg. Cardiac output was 5.2 L prior to chest pain, but was 2.1 L following chest pain. An acute anterior wall myocardial infarction was documented by EKG and cardiac enzymes over this time period.

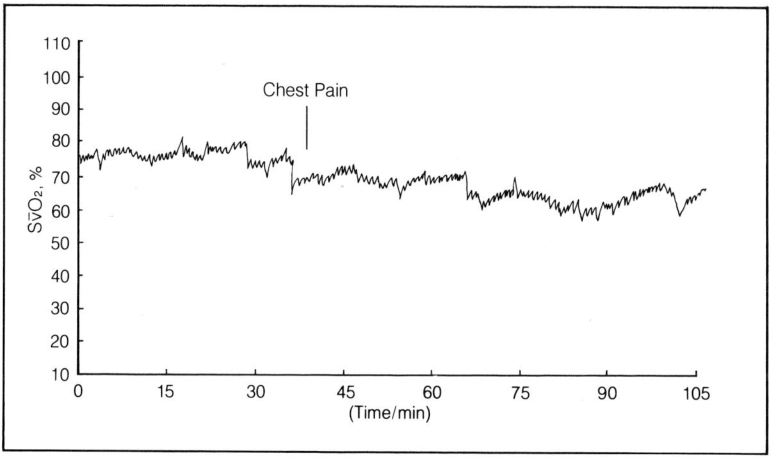

Figure 4

The 56 year old woman whose tracing is illustrated in Figure 5 had severe congestive heart failure secondary to aortic valve disease. $S\bar{v}O_2$ initially was quite low, but with titration of dobutamine infusions (20 mcg/min) $S\bar{v}O_2$ reached 75%. We found continuous $S\bar{v}O_2$ measurements very helpful in detecting abrupt changes in cardiac output and in titrating therapy with inotropic agents.

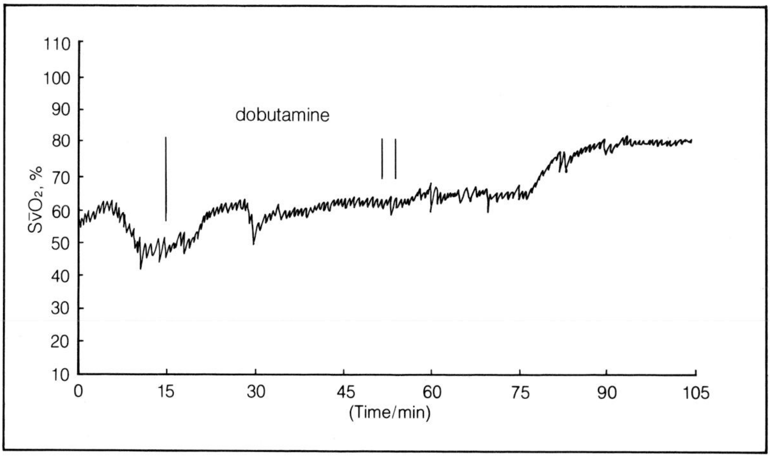

Figure 5

Oxygen Consumption Prior to using the Oximetrix pulmonary artery catheter we assumed oxygen consumption was a relatively constant number in most clinical conditions. However, we have demonstrated repeated instances of markedly increased oxygen consumption in association with seizures, shivering in the post-operative patient and in the febrile patient. The 56 year old male shown in Figure 6 was comatose and demonstrated repetitive marked decreases in $S\bar{v}O_2$ to as low as 25%! These occurred nearly every 20 minutes. Values for arterial PO_2 and cardiac output remained normal during these dramatic desaturations. Clinical correlation showed that each of these episodes accompanied a grand mal seizure. Measurement of oxygen consumption revealed an increase to greater than 500 ml/min.

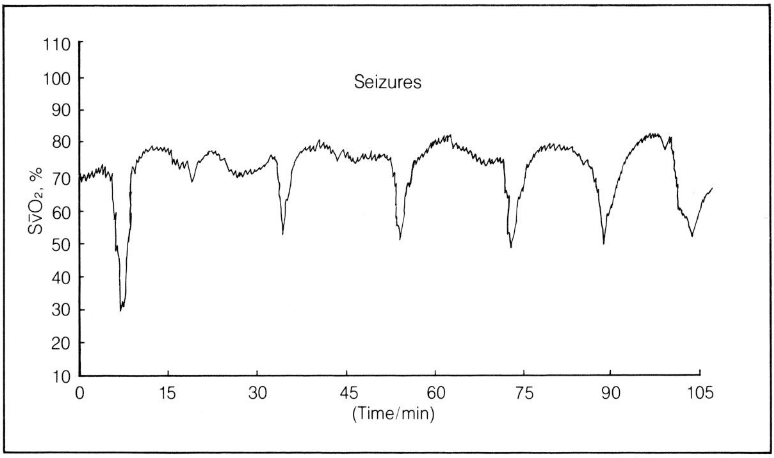

Figure 6

Repetitive seizures in the Intensive Care Unit carry a very high mortality. The dramatic effect of the increase in oxygen consumption on $S\bar{v}O_2$ may account for this high mortality.

Management of the Intensive Care Unit Patient Figure 7 illustrates a patient who experienced repetitive desaturations on 0.60 FIO_2 and 10 cm PEEP. There were no associated seizures. Instead, these desaturations were associated with aggressive tracheal suctioning. Documentation of such episodes has increased our awareness of the adverse impact of some routine procedures on critically ill patients. Greater attention to presuctioning hyperoxygenation and the use of a PEEP valve with suction adaptor has lessened these episodes.

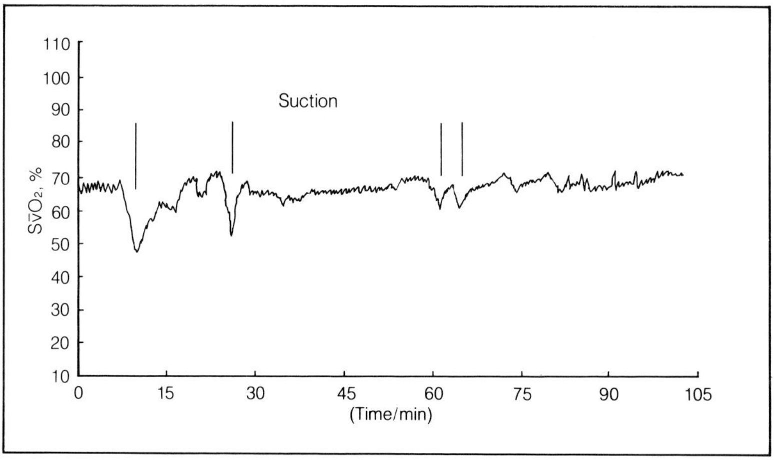

Figure 7

Body positioning can affect PO_2 in unilateral lung disease. We have been surprised by the importance of body position in patients, even with bilateral lung disease. The patient shown in Figure 8 had a decrease in $S\bar{v}O_2$ each time he was positioned on his left side. A decrease in arterial PO_2 of 20 mmHg was associated with this. How often are we unable to explain such decreases in PO_2 in a routinely obtained blood gas measurement?

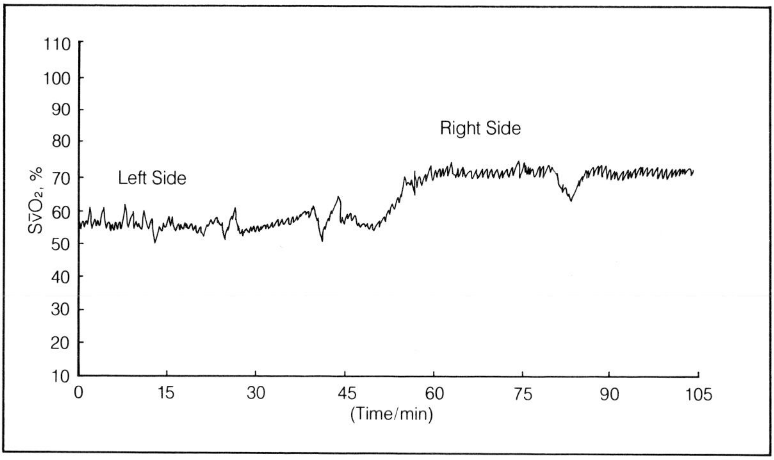

Figure 8

My last clinical scenario involves this poor fellow depicted in Figure 9, who decreased $S\bar{v}O_2$ up to 15-20% each time he got on the bedpan. Unfortunately he liked to be on the bedpan frequently during the day, so he spent a good deal of time with low $S\bar{v}O_2$ values. We did not know what to call this hypoxemia associated with being on the bedpan. While I am sure you are aware of status asthmaticus and status epilepticus, we thought this represented the first case of "status flatus."

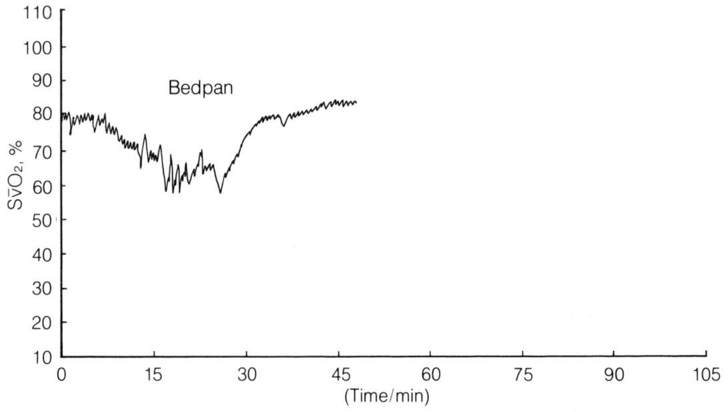

Figure 9

COST-EFFECTIVENESS

Our clinical impression was that use of this catheter lessened the need for periodic sampling of arterial blood gases. In order to examine this more carefully, we used each patient as his own control and counted the number of blood gases obtained in the 24 hours prior to catheter insertion compared to the 24 hours postinsertion, as shown in Figure 10.

FREQUENCY OF ARTERIAL BLOOD GAS STUDIES	
Pre-Opticath	Post-Opticath
7.2 ± 2.1	4.4 ± 1.6*

Results are mean ± SD and represent number of studies performed per 24 hours.

*Value significantly less than Pre-Opticath® ($p<0.05$, Student's t-test)

Figure 10

We found there was a significant reduction in the need for arterial blood gas determinations. This occurred without any special coaching or prompting of the housestaff since arterial blood gas determinations were performed based on clinical evaluation.

At Loyola University the Oximetrix pulmonary artery catheter costs approximately $80.00 more than a standard catheter. We found that this cost differential is readily made up in the first day of use because of the decreased requirement for arterial blood gas measurements. The reduction of nearly three arterial blood gas analyses per 24 hours, at $40 for each analysis, resulted in a savings of approximately $120.00 per patient studied.

In conclusion, our experience with the Oximetrix pulmonary artery catheter has been a positive one. The catheter has presented no problems with insertion. It functioned reliably and accurately for as long as was required clinically. It has improved our ability to monitor critically ill patients and at the same time has done so in a cost-effective manner.

IS CONTINUOUS MEASUREMENT OF BLOOD OXYGEN SATURATION A SIGNIFICANT ADVANCE IN HEMODYNAMIC MONITORING AND MANAGEMENT OF THE HIGH RISK PATIENT?

9

PANEL DISCUSSION
QUESTIONS AND ANSWERS

Arnold Aberman, M.D., F.A.C.P.
Patrick J. Fahey, M.D.
John W. Hoyt, M.D.
Arnold S. Leonard, M.D.
John C. McMichan, M.B., B.S., Ph.D.
Philip A. Poole-Wilson, M.D., M.R.C.P.
John F. Schweiss, M.D.
Curtis A. Sheldon, M.D.

SCHWEISS: Dr. Hoyt, don't you prefer to monitor a pressure tracing to avoid continuous wedging instead of watching a mixed venous saturation ($S\bar{v}O_2$) curve?

HOYT: Yes, of course we do. In the described situation in my presentation, the nurse thought the pressure tracing was simply a damped tracing and had not alerted the physician to it. It was only when the physician came by the bedside and noticed the change in the $S\bar{v}O_2$ recording that the whole scenario was put together. This was early on in our use of the catheter, and it certainly was embarrassing to present something where the catheter was in a wedge position for such a long period of time. We present it as just another safeguard and another clinical attribute of the catheter. But we certainly suggest attacking it earlier than that.

SCHWEISS: Dr. Leonard, what influence did temperature changes have on the accuracy of peripheral venous measurement? At our institution the Operating Rooms are maintained constantly at 68°, and the patient gets colder and colder on the periphery. As a consequence of that experience, I wonder whether temperature affects the venous oxygen saturation at all, in the periphery in these extremities?

LEONARD: In the experimental data that we had within the range of our experiment, the temperature did not vary more than 5°. Because it was a constant environment, we really did not see changes. Peripheral measurements are going to be taken of the patient very shortly, and we will have a lot better answer both under anesthesia and in the clinical setting. The reason we are interested in this area is that in smaller hospitals throughout the country there are a number of instances under anesthesia, with general surgical problems, with urologic problems and with blood loss where these parameters can be used peripherally, very nicely to reflect output: either oxygen saturation or peripheral venous oxygen pressure. These are the things that we are really trying to correlate. And also, of course, with the central area.

SCHWEISS: How large was the catheter, Dr. Leonard?

LEONARD: It was a size 20 catheter.

SCHWEISS: Dr. McMichan, please comment on the work of Dantzker et. al., (Am. Rev. Resp. 15, 122:387-395, 1980) regarding the dependence of $S\bar{v}O_2$ on oxygen consumption in the adult respiratory distress syndrome?

MCMICHAN: That's an important question. First of all, Dantzker measured mixed venous tension, not saturation. Therefore, the techniques are not truly comparable. He also used an additional complicating factor, PEEP, in some of his patients. We need to remember, that whenever we assess the measurement of $S\bar{v}O_2$, that it is not one factor that is affecting the result we are looking at. Rather, there are a number of factors. Among them is oxygen consumption. My example of the patient agitated on a mechanical ventilator demonstrates this. This patient may well have decreased arterial oxygen content associated with the ARDS. But he may also have increased oxygen consumption secondary to exercise, hyperthermia or other conditions. I do not think any of us are saying that you can infer directly what the other variables are doing from monitoring only one.

SCHWEISS: What about the need for direct measurement of cardiac output in the interpretation of $S\bar{v}O_2$?

MCMICHAN: What I am saying (and I hope my colleagues on the panel agree with me) is, if $S\bar{v}O_2$ falls into a dangerously low level, something has to be done. It may well be that this indication to do something immediately saves the patient's life. Then, you can turn around and directly measure the cardiac output, the blood gases, and if you have the facilities, the oxygen consumption to determine what was the cause of the decrease in $S\bar{v}O_2$. But the fall itself directs you to do something, immediately. And, as Dr. Schweiss said, there are different levels of where it is worrisome. But when it gets to that level, you have to do something. I think this is the most important advance in the monitoring of patients. This form of monitoring directs you to do something, now. Do not play with another machine. Do not get another set of variables. Do something. Afterward, think about what was the cause.

ABERMAN: I wonder if I can comment because Dantzker's paper made another observation. He intervened in the patient, giving PEEP, and showed that the intervention itself caused a change in oxygen consumption. This implies, thereby, that when you get a change in $S\bar{v}O_2$, it may just be related to an intervention which causes change in oxygen consumption. There is a real problem with that because, ideologically, I believe that oxygen consumption is a demand store that is set by tissue oxygen metabolic needs. It cannot be influenced very much by delivering more oxygen to the tissue unless, of course, the patient has already been in lactic acidosis accumulating oxygen debts. I would like the opinion of the rest of the panel as to whether you can actually change oxygen consumption of the body by delivering more oxygen in situations where the patient does not have an oxygen debt. Clearly, if the patient has lactic acidosis, I know you can increase oxygen consumption. I am skeptical as to whether you can increase oxygen consumption simply by delivering more oxygen, unless Dantzker's maneuver actually changed tissue metabolic needs. Then, of course, it would not surprise me. In fact, that was brought up in a letter to the American Review about Dantzker's article.

Dantzker made the point, and I still do not accept it, that simply by delivering more flow to other tissues you can increase oxygen consumption in tissue that does not have lactic acidosis. The group here has a lot of experience in monitoring. I wonder how you feel about it almost ideologically, or as a theory or a philosophy?

LEONARD: I think one way to solve that would be to put catheters in the different tissues on the venous side and then to look at the arterial side. (In fact, we are planning some of that.) Then, you would alter the situation and see if you can really, on a differential basis, change tissue beds. Because tissue beds certainly change oxygen demands. Whether you can influence just by oxygen alone, I am not sure.

ABERMAN: The problem is, of course, your intervention may actually alter the tissue's demand for oxygen.

LEONARD: Yes, that is true.

ABERMAN: And that is the problem which is very difficult to get around.

LEONARD: To avoid effects of intervention you have to have a period of stabilization, and then do your study and manipulation.

SCHWEISS: From observing a fairly large number of patients we found very frequently a fall in $S\bar{v}O_2$ in the postoperative period associated with shivering. We have now taken to administering a dose of a muscle relaxant prior to leaving the Operating Room to stabilize the patient in the initial postoperative period. We have also taken to giving them Apresoline® (hydralazine) fairly routinely. The combination kind of levels them out in the Recovery Room.

SCHWEISS: Dr. Aberman, if you have a $S\bar{v}O_2$ of 65% and a cardiac index of 1.6, do you feel that a therapeutic intervention to increase the cardiac index would be indicated?

ABERMAN: That is an important question. We saw an elderly lady who decided to sleep outdoors in Toronto one February evening. She came in with a body temperature of 28°. She was a classical case of a very low cardiac output with a good $S\bar{v}O_2$. Of course, in her case she had a very low oxygen consumption because she had very little tissue demands. I have to look at that patient and ask a fundamental question: Does the patient have lactic acidosis? If the patient with a cardiac index of 1.5 or 2 and a mixed venous saturation of 65% does not have a lactic acidosis, then, the conclusion inescapably is that the patient has sufficient oxygen to satisfy her needs. Because that is all the delivery system is there for.

There is another important point using $S\bar{v}O_2$ which I found very useful, and I do not think the speakers dwelled on it. Sometimes, it helps you pick up an error in cardiac output. If I see a patient who has a $S\bar{v}O_2$ of 75%, a cardiac output of 1.1, and a normal blood pressure, it means to me that you better repeat the cardiac output. It is hard to believe if the patient is normothermic, that there would be such a low cardiac output in the face of normal $S\bar{v}O_2$. $S\bar{v}O_2$ has another value, among its many values, in sometimes giving a hint that you have made an error in measuring cardiac output.

SCHWEISS: Dr. Aberman, do you believe that oxygen consumption-demand discrepancies are due to an inability of the tissues to utilize delivered oxygen, or do discrepancies occur because oxygen delivery is inadequate to the point that oxygen extraction drops venous oxygen to a point where the driving pressure becomes so low that the oxygen cannot be adequately transported across the cell membrane?

ABERMAN: Let us divide the question up. There are two situations to me in which you get a discrepancy between demand and consumption. You cannot look at consumption and know whether it is adequate or not without knowing what the blood lactic acid level is because if there is no lactic acidosis, the consumption is adequate. There are two situations in which you have evidences of mismatch of oxygen consumption demand with a lactic acidosis.

First, is in anemia or in particularly low cardiac output with very low $S\bar{v}O_2$. In that case, I do not think it is a problem with tissue utilizing oxygen because it was able to bring the oxygen tension to 30 Torr. Once you bring the oxygen saturation down to 30% and the tension down to 25 Torr, the tension is so low that you start having problems with diffusion gradients along to the mitochondria. That is sort of the garden variety situation, in my experience, with over 90% of the patients with a lactic acidosis.

The other example is sepsis. Patients who are septic, as Dr. Schweiss mentioned, appear to have an inability to use the oxygen. Why? Because they have the clinical syndrome of lactic acidosis, meaning mismatch of the consumption and demand; yet, their $S\bar{v}O_2$ is high. They are behaving as if they cannot use the oxygen. Now, I have grown up with three explanations to it. I just pass them on to you. I do not know which is true. First, there is a metabolic block. Oxygen is getting to the tissues, but because of sepsis and toxemia the patient cannot use the oxygen. Second, at a tissue level, they are shunting by the nutrient site. Third, there is macro-shunting. The blood flow is going to the skin which does not need the oxygen. The skin venous effluent has a high $S\bar{v}O_2$, and it is mixing with the critical tissues which have low $S\bar{v}O_2$. Does anyone know which one of those explanations is or is not right, or is there a fourth one?

MCMICHAN: The point you make about sepsis is important. I do not know which one is the mechanism. We are beginning to collect evidence now in our institution that perhaps one of the first clinical signs of the onset of sepsis is a rising $S\bar{v}O_2$ for no other apparent cause. The fact that this may be associated with tissue poisoning has been supported by work we have done using the dog model, where we give them excessively large doses of nitroprusside producing cyanide toxicity. In this situation the $S\bar{v}O_2$ also rises progressively. Once cyanide toxicity decreases cellular metabolism, it allows the oxygen to pass through into the right side of the circulation.

SCHWEISS: Dr. Poole-Wilson, were the tests described in your paper done before cardiac catheterization or before stress testing?

POOLE-WILSON: All the patients had stress testing prior to cardiac catheterization. The tests were done immediately.

Incidentally, I think the heart is a very good example of this problem. I think the way this conversation is going, these catheters are providing information which is producing problems for us. Many patients drop their $S\bar{v}O_2$ to low levels on exercise. We know it can happen in anemia. Certainly, the heart seems to run on a coronary sinus oxygen of about 30%, and I think that is probably the level which is determined by diffusion. Now, the question I would like to ask is: Why is the body unable to cope when $S\bar{v}O_2$ is 40%? There has to be some other problem. Probably it is a question of flow to body organs. There are more questions which we are going to have to ask as a result of these measurements than the answers they provide.